THE DAYS
OF HIS
PRESENCE

THE DAYS OF HIS PRESENCE

Third Printing, May 1997

Arrow Publications

P.O. Box 10102
Cedar Rapids, IA 52410
Phone: (319) 373-3011
Fax: (319) 373-3012

CONTENTS

PREFACE

I am cautious about speaking on end time events. When it comes to peering through the dark lens of prophetic anticipations, details are often obscured or exaggerated by our perspective. An additional caution is that, while we may have the same longing for the Lord's return, many of us hold differing convictions concerning the timing of end time events.

Under ideal conditions, I would first present my views to a forum of respected scholars and church leaders. In the privacy of friendship and the "spirit of the Bereans," we would study the Scriptures together **"to see whether these things were so"** (Acts 17:11).

In our day, forums of leaders actually do convene regularly over a number of issues. While I have presented the message in this book to perhaps thousands of ministers in conference settings, it is time to take this vision to the larger forum: my readers.

Although I write at times with a fervor that seems unbending, in reality I am submitting these things to you for your prayer, comments, and even opposing views. In other words, I am initiating a type of forum among us where we can seek God together.

In the last few pages, I will try to anticipate some typical questions. We will also try to respond in future editions to the most-asked questions or comments we receive. Additionally, the book is divided into five sections. I would have liked to expand these and put each under a separate cover. Tying these sections together has been difficult, as the themes in each require moving from an inspirational style to study chapters and back to inspirational. Forgive me for this inconvenience.

Finally, while we look to the Lord together about the details and specifics of these last days, to establish a strict sequence of end time events has not been my motive in writing. While we should be mindful of end time events, we must not become fearful of them; to become overly focused upon the signs of the end can be a distraction. Signs point to something bigger than themselves. Rising before us is a glorious sunrise. Let us not become so absorbed with the movement of fleeing shadows that we miss the awe of the One who is dawning upon us. Many have written about the shadows; this book is primarily about the increasing light.

For those who are truly born again—who have received the spirit of Christ in their hearts—the night is already behind us. The splendor of God is rising. My goal is to fix our vision on the light of His glory which, even now, unfolds before us.

INTRODUCTION

Several years ago, a fresh initiative came from the Holy Spirit to unite the church. For many Christians, the truth of our oneness in Christ had already become more than a theological statement. Yet, most had also accepted divisions between Christians as an unfortunate but irreversible aspect of life.

To combat this deception, the Lord not only brought an anointing to teach, He simultaneously armed many prayer warriors with a new authority in spiritual warfare. In city after city, along with the proclamation of God's Word, the ancient enemy of Christian unity, the "accuser of the brethren" was confronted (see Rev. 12:10–11).

This warfare, though far from over, has been effective. For those who doubt the veracity of strategic-level spiritual warfare, in literally thousands of cities an ever-increasing number of once-divided churches are now united in prayer, friendship, and their love of Jesus Christ.

Not only are leaders coming together, but this anointing to unify the church has become the foundation upon which a variety of powerful new ministries have emerged. Among the more visible are the March for Jesus and Promise Keepers. Without the substructure of unity, these ventures would not have reached across the broader spectrum of Christianity.

No ministry can take credit for what has come purely from the Lord's initiative. Over the past few decades many have contributed to the growing oneness among Christians. Leaders such as Jack Hayford, David Bryant, Luis Bush, E.V. Hill, John Dawson, Tony Evans, C. Peter Wagner, and Joe Aldridge have been at the forefront. Denominational directors such as Paul Cedar, Thomas Trask, and Henry Blackaby, along with many others, have been outstanding models of interdenominational prayer and interaction. Leading us all by his example has been Billy Graham, who required cooperation among churches before he would consider a local crusade.

In 1989, the Lord also initiated a new thrust to cleanse racism from the church. In these ensuing years, many citywide reconciliation services have been held around the nation and the world. The Promise Keepers movement also carries, as an integral part of its agenda, the burden to unite across racial lines.

In November of 1994, the leaders of both African-American and Caucasian streams of Pentecostal churches united in Memphis. With much weeping and godly sorrow, white leaders repented to their black brethren and received forgiveness. The outcome was that seventy years of racial separation among Pentecostals was officially ended. Out of this historic reconciliation a new organization of churches emerged called the *Pentecostal and Charismatic Churches of North America.* These denominations, once divided along ethnic lines, are now going forward united in the love of Jesus.

Following this breakthrough, in January of 1995, more than 100 white evangelical leaders from primarily non-Pentecostal churches met in Chicago with African-American church leaders, where a similar healing occurred. Then, in their 1995 annual convention in Atlanta, Southern Baptists asked for forgiveness from African-Americans for the history of racism in their denomination.

Today, church leaders, national prayer ministries, and a multitude of local pastors, intercessors, and lay workers are reaching together for a new era of Christian unity. Reconciliation between churches and races has become a growing standard for many Christians.

The stream of renewal that is rising and flowing through the body of Christ is the result of leaders returning to the **"simplicity and purity of devotion to Christ"** (2 Cor.

11:3). Our growing unity is the consequence of obedience to Jesus Christ, not compromise. Indeed, we are not compromising the truth of the gospel; we have just stopped *deifying* our preferences, methods, and cultural traditions. As we return to Jesus, each from our own background, we are finding unity with each other. We are learning that the real issue at the end of the age is not whether we follow "my way" or "your way," but Yahweh.

Because we are seeking the exaltation of Almighty God, the Holy Spirit continues to work with us as we restore Christian unity and racial harmony to biblical, New Testament standards. This was seen no clearer than in the outpouring of love and grace at the Atlanta Promise Keepers conference in February 1996. More than 40,000 ministers from a variety of backgrounds came together in prayer, repentance, and reconciliation!

I am grateful that, along with many others, God has called me to help bring healing and unity to the body of Christ. Yet what I share in *The Days of His Presence* is more compelling to me than the need to bring down sectarian divisions and racist traditions. While much work yet remains, the process of eliminating these sins is but a prelude—a preparation—for the glory of the Lord that is about to be revealed.

Part One

THE VISION

Then the Lord answered me and said,
"Record the vision
And inscribe it on tablets,
That the one who reads it may run.

"For the vision is yet for the appointed time;
It hastens toward the goal,
And it will not fail.
Though it tarries, wait for it;
For it will certainly come,
    It will not delay."
                        —Habakkuk 2:2–3

1

"One Message"

"The Lord alone will be exalted in that day."
—Isaiah 2:11

Normally my Sunday sermon is prepared a few days in advance, but this week was different. All week the heavens seemed like bronze. Saturday morning came and still I was at a loss. Nothing seemed alive. It was now Saturday evening and I was pacing the floor seeking God. *"Lord,"* I asked, *"What is the message for tomorrow morning? What topic should I address?"*

A dozen ideas filed through my mind, loitered momentarily in my imagination, and left as unanointed as they had arrived. I went to bed praying. When I woke Sunday morning, my prayer was still on my lips.

A half hour before I had to leave for church, I had not quit pacing the bedroom floor. For the umpteenth time, I asked, *"Lord, what is the message?"* when suddenly the electricity to our home clicked off, reset, and then came back on. This, in turn, caused the answering machine on my desk to also reset. Perfectly synchronized with my prayer asking for a sermon topic, the machine replied in its computerized voice:

"You . . . have . . . one . . . message."

When a voice comes out of the air and says, "You have one message," if your message is not centered upon the life and teachings of the Lord Jesus Christ, you have missed the purpose of Christianity! That morning I preached Jesus. People said there was more fire than ever in my sermon.

The fact is, the church has only one message. The proclamation of who Jesus is and what He has accomplished is the eternal message of the church; it is the only message the Father promises to confirm with power. To reveal Jesus through obedience to what He taught is to bring the life of His kingdom into our world. As we return to the simple **"purity of devotion to Christ"** (2 Cor. 11:3), we will find the most powerful manifestations of the Lord Jesus awaiting us. Indeed, at the end of the age, the church that loves Him will display Him. We will reveal His glory.

For my more traditional, evangelical friends, I should prepare you. While my primary emphasis will be strongly on the Scriptures, I also owe my views to two specific visions the Lord gave me in the beginning of my Christian experience.

Granted, I was a young disciple. Yet, so were Peter, James, and John when Jesus showed them His glory on the Mount of Transfiguration. Yes, I was unworthy and unprepared for what the Lord revealed, but what of Paul? He was not even a Christian when the glory of the Lord appeared to him. To these we can add Jacob and Joseph, David and Solomon, Isaiah and Ezekiel, Mary the mother of Jesus, and a great many others. The Lord did not require of them to be anything more than they were: people He chose for Himself while spiritually rather young. Indeed, their heavenly experiences both compelled and guided them throughout their lives.

It is scriptural for the Holy Spirit to direct young men and women to their destiny through supernatural encounters. Of course, not everyone will have such meetings, and all extra-biblical experiences should be tested against the plumb line of God's Word. Yet, we can safely say that one aspect of the Holy Spirit's work is that **"young men shall see visions"** (Acts 2:17). We are not saved by our visions, but we can be guided by them. Indeed, the Scriptures warn us: **"Where there is no vision, the people perish"** (Prov. 29:18 KJV).

When we consider that America is plagued with abortion, violence, pornography, satanism, drugs, national debt, sexual abuse, and the breakdown of the family structure, it becomes obvious we need a vision from God!

How shall we deal with the terrors that have invaded our world? Should we move to Idaho, stockpile food, and wait for the tribulation? Perhaps we should simply close our eyes to the world and hope for the rapture? Or should we find out what *God* is planning to do and throw our lives into His purpose?

My prayer is that through this book you too will receive the vision of what God is planning to do *before* Jesus comes for His elect. Everything I present here will ultimately focus us upon the one message of the church: the exaltation of the Lord Jesus Christ. We will look at what it means to be conformed to His image in the day of His power. As Jesus said, **"If you believe, you will see the glory of God"** (John 11:40). If you have faith in Christ, then come with me as we reach for the glory of God at the end of the age.

2

AT THE THRESHOLD OF GLORY

Before Jesus comes to be glorified in the earth, He is coming to be glorified in the church.

Our salvation grants us more than just church member-ship and a conservative perspective. We have, in truth, become one with Christ. The Lord Jesus is our head, we are His body; He is our husband, we are His bride; He is the vine from which we, His branches, draw our life and virtue. These images, and many more, speak openly and passionately of our eternal union with the Son of God.

Yet on a personal scale, only in the briefest of flashes have we glimpsed His mighty power working with us. We pray, we ask, we travail; but we give birth, as it were, only **"to wind"** (Isa. 26:18). Most of our sick receive just enough grace to endure suffering; they are not healed. On a national scale, only during the heights of revivals and spiritual awakenings has the church truly seen the arm of the Lord revealed and society significantly transformed.

However, as the day of Christ's return draws near, this seeming absence of power is in the process of dramatic change. Indeed, the promise of the Father to the Son, which shall be fulfilled on the highest level prior to the Lord's return, is that God's people **"will volunteer freely in the day of Thy power"** (Ps. 110:3a).

There *is* a **"day of . . . power"** at hand. Yet, not only this, but accompanying this time of power will be a glorious holiness, a radiance that will also appear upon God's people: **"In holy array, from the womb of the dawn, Thy youth are to Thee as the dew"** (Ps. 110:3b). As the day of the Lord draws near, we shall shine like the dew lit by the first rays of the millennial morning.

At the end of the age, the world will see the Lord Jesus Christ leading His church in ever-increasing displays of glory. Great power from God shall rest upon those who are choosing now to humble themselves before Him. Without hype or self-promotion, the Presence of God shall again be revealed among His people.

THE GOD OF GLORY

Nearly every Christian I know believes we are in the closing hours of this age. How close to the end, no one knows; and when Jesus will return, none presume a guess. If our hope has truly come from heaven, then the praying, hungering church of Jesus Christ is about to enter a season of extraordinary manifestations of God's glory. We are about to engage in what Bible scholars call a "dispensational" moving of God's Spirit. During such times, the Lord has *always* manifested Himself in glory.[1]

It is true that no one has seen the Father's glory, but God the Son has manifested Himself in glory numerous times in the past. Abraham saw Christ's glory while he was in Mesopotamia. Isaiah beheld Him in the year King Uzziah died. Ezekiel fell before the Living One by the river Chebar. Daniel, David, Habakkuk, Solomon, Zachariah, and Haggai all saw the glory of the Lord. *In truth, the Bible was written by people who had seen God's glory!*

Moses beheld Him, then Aaron, Nadab, Abihu, and the seventy Hebrew elders as well. Exodus tells us these men **"saw the God of Israel; and under His feet there appeared to be a pavement of sapphire, as clear as the sky itself"** (Ex. 24:10). Of their encounter with the Almighty, we read: **"and they beheld God, and they ate and drank"** (Ex. 24:11).

Think of it: *"They beheld God!"* Could anything be more wonderful? Is there not a jealousy within you for that experience—to actually gaze upon God? To behold the Lord's glory is not only scriptural, but *typical* during dispensational moves of God. The fact is, over three million Israelites saw God's glory on Mount Sinai. Young men, old women, and little children—people of every age and physical condition—all saw **"the glory of the Lord** [as it] **rested on Mount Sinai"** (Ex. 24:16)!

Yet, that unveiling of glory did not stop at Sinai. The entire Hebrew nation followed a cloud of glory by day and were illuminated by a blazing pillar of fire-like glory at night. *This happened not just once or twice but every day for forty years!* How much more shall the Lord of glory manifest Himself to us at the end of the age?

Jesus said that he who is least in His kingdom is greater than those under the old covenant (Matt. 11:11). In what ways are Christ's followers "greater"? Those in the Old Testament saw His glory from a distance, but He has chosen to reveal His glory *in* and *through* the church! Is it not written, He is coming to be **"glorified in His saints on that day, and to be marveled at among all who have believed"** (2 Thess. 1:10)?

Indeed, Jesus has not only given us His name and His words (John 17:6,14), He has also granted us to partake of His radiant splendor! The very glory which was manifest in the Old Testament, He now has deposited in the spirits of those washed and made pure in His blood. He said, **"And the glory which Thou hast given Me I have given to them"** (John 17:22).

Yes, God will again reveal His glory at the end of the age. His divine integrity requires it be so. The unsaved world will receive from God one last, legitimate opportunity to choose, not merely between the church and the sin, but between the radiance of heaven and the horrors of hell. For among those living at the end of the age, both will be manifested in fulness.

3

ARISE, SHINE!

"And it was for this He called you through our gospel, that you may gain the glory of our Lord Jesus Christ."   *—2 Thessalonians 2:14*

The Word of God states plainly—no, it commands those at the end of the age to be fearless in the face of darkness! Speaking through the prophet Isaiah, the Spirit of the Lord orders His people:

> **Arise, shine; for your light has come,**
> **And the glory of the Lord has risen upon you.**
> **For behold, darkness will cover the earth,**
> **And deep darkness the peoples;**
> **But the Lord will rise upon you,**
> **And His glory will appear upon you.**
> **And nations will come to your light,**
> **And kings to the brightness of your rising.**
>   —Isaiah 60:1–3

Traditionally, because the second half of Isaiah 60 contains references to the millennium, some have placed the fulfillment of this entire chapter in the age to come. But let

me ask: Will **"darkness . . . cover the earth"** in the millennium? During the glorious reign of Christ when death, sin,
and sorrow are banished, will **"deep darkness"** still rest on
"the peoples"? The fact is, while Isaiah's prophecy does
indeed conclude in the millennium, it *begins* during the last
hours of this age.

In the next chapter I will explain in greater detail how
I have come to believe as I do about the Lord's glory during
the end times. However, these first three verses of Isaiah 60
are clearly a pre-rapture, pre-millennial command from
God. The Lord calls us not just to endure the darkness but
to arise in His manifest glory!

Some of us feel defeated; others are worn out and
weakened by the increasing gloom in the world. Yet it is
here, where depression would otherwise capture our souls,
that we are commanded to rise. To throw off oppression is
not just an act of faith; it is an act of obedience. It is time to
cancel our plans to be miserable! Through the blood of
Christ, we break our covenant with death and darkness; we
obey the voice of our destiny!

One may argue, *But you do not know my difficulties.*
Listen to how the Amplified Bible renders the Lord's
command: **"Arise [from the depression and prostration
in which circumstances have kept you; rise to a new
life]!"** Right at this moment, even as you read these words,
new life from the Presence of God is descending into your
spirit. Receive it! Accept it! *Obey it!*

You see, God's plan is that here on earth, *in us,* the
glory of the Lord will be revealed. The luminous, radiant
light of His Presence, as it shone from Moses' face and
flooded Solomon's temple at its dedication, as it radiated
from Jesus and bathed His disciples on the Mount of Transfiguration—*that* light of God's Presence shall arise from
within us at the end of the age! This same divine glory shall,

in ever-increasing degrees of brightness, appear upon us in the years prior to the Lord's actual second coming.

In truth, this great work of grace has already begun. We are part of the Holy Spirit's expansive preparation. God is gathering together His people. We are learning to humble ourselves in repentance and prayer; we are finding friendship and unity with other Christians. Indeed, our reconciliation across denominational and ethnic barriers has an immeasurable reward attached to it. As valleys are **"lifted up, and every mountain and hill . . . made low . . . then the glory of the Lord will be revealed, and all flesh will see it together"** (Isa. 40:4–5).

God is qualifying us to receive His splendor! Nations shall come to His light and kings to the brightness of His rising!

ONLY HE IS WORTHY

Do not fear or think of yourself as unworthy—of course you are! We all are. It is for *His* glory that we are being prepared. He made no mistake in choosing you, just as He made no mistake in dying for your sins. He chose to put His Spirit within you. Personal unworthiness is not a valid excuse. Your destiny is *God's* decision. Beware lest your sense of unworthiness become a smoke screen for unbelief!

The darkness, chaos, or emptiness that may still exist in your life is not any more of a deterrent to the Almighty than the terrible, pre-creation void that awaited Him in the beginning. Certainly, your individual genesis from darkness to light shall not be too difficult for God!

Even now, the Holy Spirit is descending, hovering, and brooding over you. To your "new creation self" the voice of the Lord commands, *"Arise! Shine! Shake yourself from the depression in which circumstances have kept you! You are standing at the threshold of God's glory!"*

4

"YOU GIVE THEM SOMETHING TO EAT"

"Consequently, King Agrippa, I did not prove disobedient to the heavenly vision." —Acts 26:19

What I have come to believe concerning the Lord's glory and its manifestation in the church is supported by many Scriptures. Yet, it was through a night vision in 1971 that God granted me insight into His plan. In this spiritual encounter, I saw a great metropolis languishing under the weight of a deep and terrible darkness. Etched upon the faces of those in this wretched society was the image of hopelessness. The place was desolate of real life and the time for recovery seemed long past.

I was with a group outside the city. We were not part of the darkness, but had been "baptized" in a glorious and powerful light. During the vision, I actually experienced the power of this light surging up from my innermost being. It coursed through our hands like swords of laser light. A visible splendor shone from our bodies, especially our faces.

Suddenly, from the darkness the great multitude began to grope their way toward us. They approached, first one, then another; soon all were calling on the name of the Lord. As we laid our hands upon them and prayed for them, they also received the light.

The vision passed, and though I continued to lay in bed, I did not return to sleep. As the first light of dawn entered my bedroom window, I opened the book of Isaiah to the place where I had concluded my previous reading. There, for the first time in my young spiritual life, I read Isaiah 60. The words bolted into my eyes like lightning, then shook my insides like thunder.

I know I just quoted this verse in the last chapter, but please, let me present it again. It reads:

> **Arise, shine; for your light has come,**
> **And the glory of the Lord has risen upon you.**
> **For behold, darkness will cover the earth,**
> **And deep darkness the peoples;**
> **But the Lord will rise upon you,**
> **And His glory will appear upon you.**
> **And nations will come to your light,**
> **And kings to the brightness of your rising.**
> —Isaiah 60:1–3

It says, *"darkness will cover the earth."* This was exactly what I saw in the vision. It proclaimed, *"the Lord will rise upon you, and His glory will appear upon you."* This verse described what I had seen in the vision! It was as though I had actually stepped into the future and witnessed the fulfillment of this prophecy. The Holy Spirit and the Word, working in divine symmetry, revealed that the glory of the Lord would be manifested in His people at the end of the age. As a result, *"nations"* would come to the Lord!

Today many people are excited about the harvest and coming revival. In the early seventies and through the eighties, however, the idea of "multitudes coming to Christ" was not a common expectation. With the threat of nuclear war ever present throughout the seventies, most Christians were not thinking, praying, or acting like revival was coming.

It was against this ominous tide of fear and unbelief that the Lord spoke to me of the harvest. Today nearly one million souls a week, on the average, come to Christ from around the world. Still, even this is small compared to what God is going to do in the days ahead.

As important as the harvest is, however, the primary focus of the vision was not winning the lost; it was on the ascendancy of Christ's glory in the church. God's priority is that the Lord Jesus be lifted up: *The coming great harvest will be the result of Christ's Presence!* It will not be our programs or methods that bring this harvest into God's barns; it will be the glory of the Lord.

A THIRD WITNESS

The vision released within me lofty expectations for the future, while the text in Isaiah grounded my feet on the firm path of God's eternal Word. Still, the Lord was not done with me, and one more witness was about to come. My next reading took me to Matthew, chapter 14. As I read, I paused after verse 15. It says, **"The disciples came to Him, saying, 'The place is desolate, and the time is already past; so send the multitudes away' "** (Matt. 14:15).

This Scripture introduces the time when Jesus miracu-lously fed the multitudes. As I read, I noticed similarities between the vision of the multitudes in darkness and this scene from the gospels. Both scenes depicted a place of desolation and both communicated the sense that the situation was beyond remedy. Yet in spite of the apparent hopelessness of each, multitudes were ministered to in both.

Of course, there was no theological connection between the two texts; not even the most imaginative Christian would ever reference Matthew 14:13–21 with Isaiah 60:1–3. Yet, the Lord was speaking something deep into my heart. The text continues:

> **Jesus said to them, "They do not need to go away; you give them something to eat!"**
>
> **And they said to Him, "We have here only five loaves and two fish." And He said, "Bring them here to Me."**
>
> **And ordering the multitudes to recline on the grass, He took the five loaves and the two fish, and looking up toward heaven, He blessed the food, and breaking the loaves He gave them to the disciples, and the disciples gave to the multitudes.** —Matthew 14:16–19

Jesus had taken bread, blessed it, and then broken it. Again, I paused. This time it was because of a peculiarity concerning my last name: in Italian, *Frangipane* actually means "to break bread." I wondered, was the Lord using the meaning of my name to somehow connect the feeding of the multitudes with the multitudes I saw in the vision?

Later that morning, I related the vision and the Lord's promise from Isaiah to my wife, Denise. I then told her about the feeding of the five thousand. I mentioned how I felt, that, during the time of the end, when the world would seem utterly desolate and lost, the Lord would use us like He used the loaves to feed the multitudes. Then, in an effort to truly amaze her, for the first time in our young married life I explained that our last name, *Frangipane,* meant "to break bread." It was at that point my wife told me the meaning of her maiden name, *Piscitelli.* It meant "little fishes."

LITTLE IS MUCH WITH JESUS

For the next three days I was so caught up with God I felt like my spirit was practicing for the rapture. Like Noah, Abraham, Moses, and many others in the Bible, long before we even knew the Lord, He had confirmed His eternal purpose with us in the very meaning of our names!

Between the vision, the text in Isaiah, and the meaning of our names, I am convinced that a period of great glory and harvest awaits the church. Through the account of Christ's feeding the multitudes, the Lord also warned us to expect sincere but weary disciples to try to dampen our spirits. When Christians complain that the time of the harvest **"is already past,"** or that society has become too **"desolate,"** it would be an error for any of us to ask Christ to **"send the multitudes away."** The Lord has made it plain: it willl not be too late or desolate for Him.

The Lord has proven many times that, as Christians, we do not need to stockpile resources before we attempt the "impossible." As long as we remain "blessed and broken" in the hands of the Master, our few loaves and fish are enough. What we have learned is that Jesus does not need a lot to work His miracles; He just requires we give Him all we have.

SCRIPTURE CANNOT BE BROKEN

To my wife and I, the prophetic meanings attached to our last names tell us that the purposes of God are preordained. However, for all that these things mean to us personally, it is upon the Scriptures that faith must rest. Dreams, visions, and supernatural "coincidences" are still subjective experiences which must be confirmed and established by the written word of God. We rest upon God's word because Jesus said, **"Scripture cannot be broken"** (John 10:35).

Again He said, **"Do not think that I came to abolish the Law or the Prophets; I did not come to abolish, but to fulfill"** (Matt. 5:17). This is a most profound thought: *The Scriptures cannot be broken, they can only be fulfilled!*

The Lord assures all of us: **"So shall My word be which goes forth from My mouth; it shall not return to Me empty, without accomplishing what I desire, and without succeeding in the matter for which I sent it"** (Isa. 55:11).

Regardless of the current spiritual condition of Christianity, every promise God has made concerning His glory in the church, His wrath upon the nations, His purpose with Israel, and the harvest at the end of the age—every word will have its day of fulfillment! With the Almighty, it is never a matter of *if* His word will come to pass but *when* and *with whom.* For just as God cannot cease being God, so Scripture cannot be broken.

It matters not that the hour is late or that our cities are desolate, Jesus is still saying, *The multitudes do not need to go away.* As little qualified as we Christians may consider ourselves, if we truly give our all to Christ, He will bless us and break us, and then fill us with glory to reach multitudes. Indeed, He says to each of us, *You give them something to eat.*

5

THE INTENSIFYING PRESENCE

"He is the sole expression of the glory of God—the Light-being, the out-raying of the divine—and He is the perfect imprint and very image of [God's] nature, upholding and maintaining and guiding and propelling the universe by His mighty word of power."
—*Hebrews 1:3* AMPLIFIED

The surest way to know the heart of God is by studying His word. If we are willing to simply obey what the Bible commands, we will never fall short of God's glory; we will find the place of His Presence.

Yet, even as we avow that full obedience to the Scriptures is our highest priority, in these last days other forms of communication can, and will, come to us from God. The Holy Spirit may use dreams, visions, and spiritual gifts to help us toward our future (1 Cor. 12:7–11; Acts 2:17).

In the previous chapter, I presented the vision of the last hours of this age as it was shown me by the Lord. I know that I only saw a glimpse of one aspect of the end times. Like you, I also know the unrepentant world is destined for the Great Tribulation, and that many worldly Christians will become spiritual prisoners of the Antichrist. But as far as the living, praying church is concerned, if we continue to climb toward the standard of Christlikeness, ahead of us lies a time of great glory and harvest. To this vision of glory and harvest, let me submit to you a second encounter I had with the Lord, which occurred about two years after the first.

T he year was 1973. I was pastoring a small church in Hilo, Hawaii, and had been in a month of intense prayer and extended fasting. It was an earnest time of drawing near to God. At the end of this period, I found myself awakened during the night by a visitation of the Lord. It was not as though I saw His physical features; I saw His glory and was overwhelmed by His Presence.

Immediately I was like a dead man, unable to move so much as a finger. Spiritually, however, the heavens unveiled before me without boundaries. My state of awareness was heightened beyond anything I have ever known. I felt like one of those **"living creatures"** in the book of Revelations, as though I possessed **"eyes around and within"** (Rev. 4:8).

With my "inner eyes" I discovered the truth about my righteousness. Remember, I felt close to the Lord. I thought my spiritual condition was fine. Yet, I suddenly became aware of my *true* human condition. The flaws in my life became unbearably vivid and utterly sinful. I saw my iniquity not as something I occasionally committed but as something I perpetually was.

I became instantly aware of the many times I could have been more loving or kind or sensitive. I also saw how selfish nearly all of my actions were. Yet, for all that was resident within me of unrighteousness, I felt no rebuke from the

Lord, nor condemnation. No voice came from heaven to convict me of my wrongs. The only voice condemning me was my own; in the light of His Presence, I abhorred myself (see Job 42:6 KJV).

Without any buffer of self-justification or deceit, with no other person but God to whom to compare myself, I saw how far short of His glory I truly was. I knew why mankind needed the blood of Christ. And I knew that no amount of personal attainment in and of itself could ever make me like Jesus. In the most profound way I understood that only Christ could live like Christ. God's plan was not to improve me but to remove me so that the Lord Jesus Himself could actually live His life through me (Gal. 2:20). In His indwelling would rest my hope of becoming like Him.

I observed things that were intimately personal. And I also gained an understanding of Christ's expansive Presence and the impact His glory will have on the church at the end of the age. In what seemed to be a far distant night sky, I witnessed the most glorious, heavenly procession. The divinely "electrified" atmosphere which I felt in my bedroom was being broadcast from this very distant passage of supernatural beings.

In the forefront were pairs of magnificent angels: archangels, cherubim, seraphim, thrones, and dominions. There were angels of every class and order. Each pair was uniquely clothed in a radiant splendor all its own.

About one third of the way back was the Lord. The light of His glory was like the sun in the midst of a string of beautiful, multicolored stars. Behind Him were innumerable saints, but I could not see clearly into the Lord's glory; His brightness so enveloped those following Him, it was as though they had become a part of His being. It was obvious that the brilliance which illuminated the entire procession issued from Him.

I realized that the Lord was not just coming to judge the earth but to fill the earth with His glory. I cannot tell you in words about this glory but, even though the Lord was so far away, the radiance of His Presence was like a living fire upon my consciousness. The energy was almost painful.

Then, without warning, the procession came closer, not just to me but—I am convinced—also to this world. It was as though a mark in time or a spiritual boundary had been crossed. Instantly, my spiritual consciousness became so overwhelmed by the intensity of the Lord's Presence that I could not—no, not for another moment—bear the increase of His glory. I felt as though my very existence would be consumed by the blast furnace of His radiance.

In the deepest prayer I have ever uttered, my entire being begged the Lord to return me to my body. Suddenly, mercifully, I was cocooned once again in the familiar world of my senses and my bedroom.

Night passed into dawn and I rose early, dressed, and went outside. With each step, I pondered the vision. The Lord brought my attention to the sun as it ascended above the eastern horizon. As I looked, I saw parallels between the radiance of the sunlight and the glory of the Lord. I realized in a new way that **"the heavens are telling of the glory of God"** (Ps. 19:1).

I saw that even though the sun is 93 million miles from the earth, we feel its heat and live in its light. It is inconceivably far away, yet its energy is also here. It warms us and in its light our life exists.

So also the expanse of the Lord's Presence emanates from His glorified body in heaven. Physically, He is distant, yet at times we actually feel the out-raying of His Presence here; we are, in truth, warmed by His love.

The glory of Christ, like the out-raying of the sun, is "safe" as long as He remains distant from us in heaven. But imagine if, with each successive decade, the sun were to steadily move closer to the earth. Radiation, heat, and light would increase dramatically. With each stage of its approach, the world as we know it would radically change!

So also will this world change as the person of the Lord Jesus and His millennial reign draw near. The radiance of His Presence will increasingly fill the spiritual realms surrounding our world. And not only will the world as we know it begin to experience dramatic changes as demonic strongholds are confronted and toppled by the Lord, but among those whose hearts are open and longing for Him, a great transformation will occur!

If the sun drew closer, the increasing heat and light would soon be all we would think about. While the righteous are experiencing **"glory and honor and peace"** from His Presence (Rom. 2:10), the same glory will cause terrible **"tribulation and distress"** to the unrepentant world (v. 9). The wicked will cry to the mountains and rocks, **"Fall on us and hide us."** From what? **"the *Presence* of Him"** (Rev 6:16, *italics mine*). As the Lord's nearness increasingly intensifies, the hearts of the irreconcilable will harden like Pharaoh's.

Yet the same sun that hardens the clay also melts the butter. So, as He draws nearer, the prayer of the righteous will be, *Fill us with the Presence of the Lamb!* The Presence of Christ will be all that fills our minds. Those who love Him will experience the increase of His pleasure; they will taste the nectar of heaven. Whether we are for or against the Lord, everyone's mind will be flooded with thoughts about God.

"For behold, the day is coming, burning like a furnace; and all the arrogant and every evildoer will be chaff; and the day that is coming will set

them ablaze," says the Lord of hosts, "so that it
will leave them neither root nor branch.

"But for you who fear My name the sun of
righteousness will rise with healing in its wings;
and you will go forth and skip about like calves
from the stall.

"And you will tread down the wicked, for they
shall be ashes under the soles of your feet on the
day which I am preparing," says the Lord of
hosts.   —Malachi 4:1–3

Simultaneously two events will manifest from one
eternal source. The same increasing Presence causes wrath
to descend upon the wicked, while glory rises and is seen
upon the righteous. For we who fear the Lord, the **"sun of
righteousness"** will rise with healing in its rays.

SAME JESUS, NEW SPLENDOR

When Christ returns to this world, He is coming clothed
in the splendor of the Father (Mark 8:38). My prayer is that
each of us will perceive this reality: it is *God* Himself who
is drawing near to earth! Habakkuk, the prophet, gives us an
awesome view into the actual day when the Lord reveals
Himself to the world. He wrote:

God comes from Teman, and the Holy One from
Mount Paran. Selah. His splendor covers the
heavens, and the earth is full of His praise.

His radiance is like the sunlight; He has rays
flashing from His hand, and there is the hiding
of His power.   —Habakkuk 3:3–4

There will be a time when the Lord Jesus actually is
revealed in the heavens. In that final moment His splendor

will literally flood the skies like **"the sunlight."** Every eye will see Him with power flashing like terrible bolts of lightning from His hands.

Yet, *before He appears,* while He is near but still invisible, that same radiance of glory will be poured out on **"all flesh"** (Acts 2:17–21). For as He is in power and glory when He appears, so He is beforehand though unseen! And it is this out-raying Presence which will grow ever more resplendent in the church prior to His second coming.

With each surge of His glory many things will be quickened on earth. Satan, and the nations under him, will rage against the Lord and His purposes. Demonically-manipulated social and ethnic upheaval will intensify, increasing lawlessness, rebellion, and hopelessness in the world. The earth itself will suffer as droughts, and air and water pollution, cause unpredictable and, in many cases, disastrous changes in the patterns of life. There will be earthquakes in regions where earthquakes were unknown. Coastal cities will have mass evacuations, for there will be **"dismay among nations, in perplexity at the roaring of the sea and the waves"** (Luke 21:25).

At the same time, we who are open and yielded to Christ will watch in amazement as His Presence *in us* also intensifies and increases! He will invade our thoughts, plunder our unbelief, and purge our carnality. He will present to Himself a bride without spot or wrinkle or any such thing.

The church will be beautified with His glory and filled with His radiance *before* He physically comes for her! A time will come when our repentance and reconciliation will be complete. At that time the Scripture will be fulfilled that the bride of Christ **"has made herself ready"** (Rev. 19:7). The church will find in Christ a new level of holiness and purity which will manifest in a radiance that is both **"bright and clean"** (v. 8).

Many promises given to the church, formerly thought impossible, will be fulfilled by the fulness of Christ in us. The days ahead will be seasons of glory. The Shekinah Presence of Christ, as He is enthroned upon the praises of His people, will manifest and abide in unfading glory. We have not yet seen worship services like those that await us in the future. The day is coming when the command of the worship leaders shall be to **"make His praise glorious"** (Ps. 66:2)! A spiritual majesty will accompany the worshipers of God. Even among the most simple peoples of earth, those who love God will be companioned by His royal Presence.

In the most profound ways, the magnificence of the Lord will unfold before us. We will marvel at how God has humbled and brought low the kings of the earth. But one King shall ever rise in prominence. To Him every knee will bow! And while we too shall bow at His splendor, our highest joy shall be that we have personally known Him!

As each new level of glory arrives and unfolds, the Holy Spirit will require fresh and frequent examinations of our relationship with Christ. Whether our backgrounds are evangelical or charismatic, traditional or Pentecostal, *all who love the Lord will change.* For whatever inhibits the fusion of our lives with Christ will be consumed like chaff in the fire of His Presence.

In this season of transformation, we will know Him both in the fellowship of His sufferings and in the power of His resurrection. We will know the fulness of Christ. And it shall come to pass—not because of our righteousness but because of His increasing fulness. He *must* increase and we *must* decrease until His Presence fills everything, everywhere, with Himself.

Part Two

THE PRESENCE
OF GOD

*He made known to us the mystery
of His will . . . with a view to an
administration suitable to the fulness
of the times, that is, the summing up
of all things in Christ, things in the
heavens and things upon the earth.*
                    —*Ephesians 1:9–10*

6

In the Fulness of the Times

God has but one goal for all of creation: for every Christian, every church, and even the world itself, His ultimate objective is the consummation of all things in Christ.[1]

To the ancients, the long flat sequence of repetitive events which we know as *time* also had unique seasons of astonishing and rapid change. The Greeks used the word *kairos* to describe these special seasons. The word has no English equivalent, but "kairos" referred to that rare period when the world's direction was dramatically altered by foreordained events or great accomplishments.

When the word *kairos* was used in the New Testament, it spoke of age-changing transitions. During kairos times, the Lord transcends the boundaries of His spiritual

---

[1] The four chapters in Part Two probe some of the original Greek wording of the Scriptures. The writing style in these study chapters requires a shift on the reader's part.

laws—those self-governing life principles which punish or reward mankind accordingly. To a certain degree, the Lord actually unveils Himself, showing His power through signs and wonders as well as through the words and actions of His servants.

Paul referred to this special era as the **"fulness of the times"** (Eph 1:10; Gal 4:4). It is important to note that this period of divine activity is an *extended* time frame lasting several scores of years. These years involve a period of preparation in which God's servant is prepared, which in turn leads to an accelerated but shortened season of increased spiritual activity. The kairos time finally fades several decades into the new dispensation.

Noah and Moses served God during the kairos times spanning two ages. Noah was 100 years building the ark, while Moses and Israel spent approximately seventy-five years from the Exodus to the passing of Joshua's generation in the Promised Land.

The New Testament begins with such a time. The Scriptures tell us that, **"when the fulness of the time (kairos) came, God sent forth His Son"** (Gal. 4:4). This epoch continued well into the end of the first century. Paul wrote to the Ephesians in approximately A.D. 62 speaking of the kairos time, which he believed would consummate with the return of Christ (Eph. 1:10). At that point, this season of heightened spiritual activity had lasted over sixty years. By definition, the kairos time could be said to include the entire apostolic era during which the New Testament Scriptures were written and Christ's ministry and message proclaimed.

It is unfortunate that, when we think of the end of the age, we have traditionally limited the period of divine activity to the seven tribulation years expected at Christ's return.[1] This shorter season indeed represents the very end of all things. And while it is truth that kairos times also represent the *peaks* of spiritual activity that occur between ages, the biblical pattern tells us that there is a longer period of preparation, miracles, and ever-increasing spiritual fulness that exists for God's servants *prior to* the consummation of the age.

The generations alive during these seasons of change either become people of destiny or people dedicated to great calamity. It is a time when the gray compromise between good and evil evaporates. Evil manifests in thick darkness, while righteousness ascends to its most radiant and awesome heights.

CENTURY OF CHANGE

I believe the world has been in an unfolding kairos time for nearly 100 years. Indeed, within this past century, mankind has undergone more rapid and sweeping changes and, certainly, more technological advances, than have occurred in all accumulative history. Consider also this era has been highly *prophetic* with dozens of fulfilled Scriptures—all describing the conditions forecast for the time of the end!

The changes in our century have been spectacular! We stood amazed as seventy years of Soviet Communism crumbled. Yet this pales when we consider there are those among us today who witnessed the collapse of the 4,000-year-old Chinese dynasties, the 1,100-year-old Japanese imperial kingdoms, and the 400-year-old Czarist empires of Russia!

During the vast majority of man's history, change occurred so slowly that one or two major events would influence a nation for decades. In Peter's day, people challenged the idea of world-altering change. It was common to mock: **"Where is the promise of His coming? For ever since the fathers fell asleep, all continues just as it**

was from the beginning of creation" (2 Peter 3:4). If we return to Solomon's era, life's basic tenor was likewise predictable. Solomon perceived that there was **"nothing new under the sun"** (Eccl. 1:9).

Even though the early disciples lived in their own unique kairos period, because they thought they were at the end of the age they *expected* their kairos time to culminate in the return of Christ. Because of these delayed expectations, criticism rose against the early disciples. Scoffers, observing the unchanging rule of the Roman Empire, taunted, **"all continues just as it was."**

For us, however, very few things have remained the same during this past century. No one would be foolish enough to criticize our last hundred years for proceeding without change!

This phenomenon of continual change was predicted by the prophet Daniel as a sign of the end. Looking through the dark corridors of time, the Spirit of God identified two significant beacons to warn mankind that he had entered the last hours of the age. He said, **"many shall run to and fro"** and **"knowledge shall be increased"** (Dan. 12:4 KJV). Certainly, increased travel and knowledge epitomize mankind's greatest advances.

Consider: we routinely jet through the skies at speeds once thought inconceivable to our ancestors. In just two hours of air travel we cover what formerly took five months to accomplish on land! Likewise, mankind's accumulative knowledge of his world doubles every two years, and the rate is increasing. We not only have access to libraries of information, we have information highways. Through the use of computers, fiber optics, and the Internet, new scientific breakthroughs are transferred between individuals instantly.

Yet, in spite of technological advances, the most hideous crimes against mankind have also multiplied during our century. Millions of mothers actually pay to have their offspring killed through abortion. In the larger cities, murder is so common that only the most bizarre cases capture the media's attention. Thus another prophecy is coming to pass before our eyes: **"Because lawlessness is increased, most people's love will grow cold"** (Matt. 24:12). Truly, the love of many has grown cold.

Like never before in history, our century has seen another warning from Jesus fulfilled. He predicted that **"nation will rise against nation, and kingdom against kingdom"** (Matt. 24:7). The first world war had over 10 million deaths and 20 million wounded! World War II engaged every major world power in the conflict. After two devastating world wars and various attempts at global peace, bloody conflicts continue to sweep millions to death and destruction. For all our prosperity, the world has seen a continuous escalation in crime and rebellion, far beyond mankind's capacity to mete out justice.

Additionally, the wantonness and irresponsibility of those harvesting the wealth of the earth has caused the planet to be **"polluted by its inhabitants"** (Isa. 24:5). Thus, **"a curse devours the earth, and those who live in it are held guilty"** (v. 6). We are plagued with acid rain, polluted air, depleted ozone, and undrinkable rivers. Pesticides and herbicides have contaminated our soil. Christians seem indifferent to the needs of the environment. They forget that the earth is the Lord's. Yet, when God's judgment is executed, He will **"destroy those who destroy the earth"** (Rev. 11:18).

THE GREATEST PORTENTS

Certainly, one of the most compelling signs of the times is the restoration of Israel as a nation. Never have so many people, so long removed from their homeland, been restored as a nation. Yet in 1948, after almost 1,900 years of exile, Israel was re-established in her land. By itself, this is one of the most significant end time events to come to pass in our day, literally fulfilling dozens of prophecies (see Jer. 16:14–15; Ezek. 36; Amos 9:14–15).

The return of the Jews to Israel is profound in light of Jesus' prophecy in Luke 21:24. He said that Israel will **"fall by the edge of the sword, and will be led captive into all the nations; and Jerusalem will be trampled under foot by the Gentiles until the times of the Gentiles be fulfilled."** In 1967, after 2,500 years of oppression and foreign domination, the whole of Jerusalem was again in Jewish hands! We are rapidly coming to an end of the **"times of the Gentiles!"** [2]

Another weighty and wonderful fulfillment of the last days has to do with the harvest, which Jesus said would occur at **"the end of the age"** (Matt. 13:39). Even while you read this, the greatest gathering of souls the world has ever seen is occurring. According to the U.S. Center for World Missions, based on the rate compiled between 1990 and 1995, every day approximately 140,000 souls worldwide are brought into the kingdom of God!

Consider also the publishing of the Word of God. From Christ's birth to the year A.D. 500, nine translations of the Scriptures were completed. During the next 1,400 years, thirty additional languages were added. But since 1900, the Bible has been published in over 1,000 languages! [3]

What we are seeing fulfilled in our days is nothing less than another kairos, or fulness of times. The very contours of life as we have known it are being stretched to accommodate the invasion of God! And if, indeed, we are in the fulness of time, then the final season of power and glory is just ahead!

7

ALL THINGS
IN CHRIST

*The goal of God for the church is nothing less than
the fulness of Christ in the fulness of the times.*

I n the previous chapter we spoke of the spiritual fulness,
the kairos time, that many church leaders believe we are
currently in. We mentioned that there were three other times
in the Bible when similar periods of heightened spiritual
activity occurred: the years surrounding Noah, Moses, and
the Lord Jesus. Historically, these intervals have lasted from
70 to 100 years.

To prosper during the season between epochs, we must
grasp what the Lord seeks to accomplish during this time.
The same way Noah knew beforehand that God was going
to flood the world with water, so we need to understand that
at the end of the age God is going to flood the earth with His
glory. He will not only manifest His glory in the judgments
He executes against the wicked, but also in His righteousness that is revealed among His people (Rev. 19:8). How we

prepare for His glory during these days will determine the measure of either our blessedness or regret in the days of His Presence.

THE TRANSCENDENT PURPOSE

For many, God's manifold purpose at the end of the age is shrouded in mystery and fear. Straining to see prophetically into the dimly lit future, we almost automatically focus on the two most powerful end time events: the rapture or the fearsome days of the tribulation. Even theologians, however, divide over which will arrive first in the destiny of the church.

Yet, the Lord revealed a glorious secret to Paul. There was still another dimension to the divine, end time purpose which the early church embraced: *the unfolding of glory among God's people.* This revelation was at the substructure of much of Paul's teaching concerning the last days. In a very unique way, the Lord had granted Paul **"a view to an administration suitable to the fulness of the times"** (Eph. 1:10). In his epistle to the Ephesians, Paul presented what he called **"the mystery of [God's] will . . ."** (v.9) which he believed would be revealed during **"the fulness of the times"** (v.10).

What exactly was this mystery destined to unfold at the end of the age? It was nothing less than **"the summing up of all things in Christ, things in the heavens and things upon the earth"** (Eph. 1:10).

When the apostle speaks of God summing up heavenly and earthly **"things"** in Christ, he does not see this as a *singular* event but a *process* of many interconnected prophetic fulfillments which, in turn, lead to the culmination of all things in Christ.

Indeed, when Paul speaks of this **"summing up"** of all things, the Greek word he chose was originally an accounting term. It referred to the familiar method of addition: adding one item to another to get a sum total.

Similarly, Paul is speaking of the progression of prophetic fulfillments in the next verse, stating, **"we who were the first to hope in Christ should be to the praise of His glory"** (Eph. 1:12).

He says that this divine, universal transformation began with the first century church. Yet, obviously, they did not experience the completion of that process. Thus, the *fulfillment* of what began with them will be reinitiated in earnest with the church alive at the end of the age! And, we can expect that this administration of God's purpose will be displayed as a mighty work of grace; one which, as Paul stated, would be **"suitable to the fulness of the times"** (Eph. 1:10).

In other words, just as we have been awed by the changes in the world over the last century, so will we be awed by the continual unfolding manifestation of Christ in the true church (see 2 Thess. 1:10)!

Paul put a headline over this entire period of end time transformation: he called it **"the fulness of the times."** Again, the word here for "times" is *kairos.* This season is not only significant, it is destined to contain **"the fulness"** of significance and divine accomplishment. What awaits the church is an unparalleled intensification of divine activity. This activity, among other things, will fill the true church, Christ's bride, with glory in preparation for Christ's second coming (see Rev. 19:7–8).

The primary end time events with which the church has been concerned focused on the "great falling away," the "perilous times," the "tribulation" and the "rapture." Yet, God also granted Paul this awesome **"view"** into the **"administration"** of glory at the end of the age!

The word translated *administration* is elsewhere in the New Testament rendered "stewardship." It not only refers to God taking the initiative to bring His creation back into order, but reveals that, in His sovereignty, He has chosen to include His servants in various degrees in that process!

Paul says that the church at the end of the age is being granted a stewardship, a mandate from heaven. At the bidding of the Sovereign King, we are called to participate with God in the process of divine consummation, a process that starts with us being consumed in our love and surrender to Christ!

For the unrepentant world, the apostate church, and the demons of hell, this will manifest as a period of God's judgment and wrath. However, for those who are yielded to God, the same Spirit which comes to judge the wicked is also coming to inhabit and transform the righteous!

Paul perceived that this end time partnership between Christ and the overcoming church would release the most spectacular execution of God's power. It would not just be divine intervention, but divine *assimilation:* **"the summing up of all things in Christ, things in the heavens and things upon the earth."**

THE ETERNAL PICTURE

The apostolic writers of the New Testament expected they would experience the consummation of the age (see 1 Cor. 10:11, Heb. 9:26, etc.). Their writings were truly inspired by God, even if their sense of timing was premature. Thus, Paul's view of the first century church is actually *God's* view of the last century church!

As modern Christians, we have tended to glorify the first century church and remove ourselves from any comparison to it. Yet, it is imperative that we understand there is another **"fulness of times"** due the church during the last decades of the age. This kairos time will *exceed* in power what was experienced by the early Christians; in this final period all things *will* be consummated in Christ!

It is right that we should apply Paul's expectations for the first century church to ourselves. We must realize that God's purpose with us will not be over until the entire created universe is also consummated in Christ. Paul recognized the church was the first fruits of this universal consummation (see also James 1:17–18). Indeed, this vision of Christ's unfolding fulness in the church was the foundational truth of Paul's most sublime teachings.

He speaks of having died with Christ and of Christ now living within him (Gal. 2:20); he tells us that in baptism we are literally clothed with Christ (Gal. 3:27). To the Romans he explains the church has been predestined to become conformed to Christ, and toward this magnificent purpose all things are currently working (Rom. 8:28–29; Eph. 1:11).

Paul is speaking of this progressive summing up of all things in Christ in his letter to the Corinthians. Listen to Paul's end time vision: **"But we all, with unveiled face beholding as in a mirror the glory of the Lord, are being transformed into the same image from glory to glory, just as from the Lord, the Spirit"** (2 Cor. 3:18). Once again we find the church entering Christ's glory in successive stages of fulness.

Paul is not only identifying the normal sequence of Christian growth, he is actually referring to the bigger picture: the progressive consummation of the church in Christ! He perceived the church as being absorbed into Christ **"from glory to glory."** He says, **"we all . . . behold . . . the glory of the Lord."** Paul saw the living church **"being transformed"** in an unfolding process that would culminate in the return of Christ and then the final summing up of all things in Him.

In the very next verse, the apostle says, **"Therefore, since we have this ministry"** (2 Cor. 4:1). What ministry? Paul sees his mission not only as a teacher, but as one sent by God to establish the church in Christ's glorious Presence at the end of the age!

Just as Moses stood in the actual Presence of God and, consequently, reflected the Lord's glory, so shall the Lord again descend into our lives in awesome, transforming splendor! This unfolding of glory shall not end until our bodies are changed and all creation is filled with the Spirit of Christ!

To these Corinthians, Paul reinforces the concept that this end time administration is an *unfolding process* that shall carry us **"from glory to glory, just as from the Lord, the Spirit"** (2 Cor. 3:18). God is beginning this process with those in this generation who are **"the first to hope in Christ."** The outcome is that our lives, just as those in the first century, **"should be to the praise of His glory"** (Eph. 1:12).

THE APOSTOLIC PRAYER

Paul knew that deep, intractable faith in the divine plan would not come only by explanation; the church needed revelation as well. Thus, after unveiling God's purpose of summing up all things in Christ, Paul then prayed to **"the Father of** [the coming] **glory"** to grant believers **"a spirit of wisdom and of revelation in the knowledge of Him"** (Eph. 1:17). Why? So that as Christians, alive during momentous, prophetic times, each of us would know **"what is the hope of His calling, what are the riches of the glory of His inheritance in the saints"** (v. 18).

Let us, even now, honestly examine our view of God's end time plan. *Do we know the hope of His calling? Has it been revealed to us what are the riches of glory which are our inheritance?* As Paul prayed for the church in the first century, let us also pray, not just for information, but revelation, concerning the destiny of the church at the end of the age.

Father, reveal to my heart what You are doing both in me and in the church in this hour! I know You are uniting and reconciling us to each other, but show me the hope of my calling. Reveal to my heart the riches of Your glory in the saints! In Jesus' name. Amen.

The first century was but the anticipation of what is yet to occur with the church at the end of the age. There remains one last great outpouring of the Holy Spirit. It will be a time when everything God revealed to Paul will come to pass! During this last great time of fulness, the Presence of Christ will expand in the lives of those surrendered to His Lordship. All that Paul expected to occur among the first century saints will be fulfilled with us during the last years before Christ returns.

Indeed, this period will far exceed what was accomplished in the first church. For during the days of the last church, what Jesus paid for at Calvary shall be purchased: All things shall be consummated in Christ. During this time, we who have put our hope in Christ shall be to the praise of His glory. We will know the fulness of Christ in the fulness of the times.

8

THE
MORNING STAR

"They looked expectingly unto Him, and they became bright." ———*Psalm 34:5 YOUNG*

Nowhere in the Bible is the idea expressed that when an age changes, it does so rapidly. Certainly, there may be sudden, unanticipated events in the process of change. But when Paul warns that the day of the Lord will come **"like a thief in the night"** (1 Thess. 5:2), it is only in the minds of sinners, apostates, and the spiritually unprepared that the Lord arrives without warning.

Paul qualifies his remarks about the Lord's return in his very next thought: **"But you, brethren, are not in darkness, that the day should overtake you like a thief; for you are all sons of light and sons of day. We are not of night nor of darkness"** (1 Thess. 5:4–5). For those who are obedient to Christ, the day does not come suddenly, but steadily.

The phrase, "the day of the Lord," represents the millennium age when Jesus reigns and God's glory covers the earth. When that day fully dawns, Jesus shall bring with Him a splendor so great it shall illuminate the entire city of God, an area with a perimeter of 1,500 miles (Rev. 21:16). We will never again need the light of the sun nor any lamp!

Yet, even while we are in this present age, Paul says that *now* we are **"sons of light and sons of day."** We are a hybrid people, born of the flesh in one age, but alive in the Spirit of the age to come!

Jesus Himself admonishes us, **"While you have the light, believe in the light, in order that you may become sons of light"** (John 12:36). Right now we are **"sons of light."** As such, we **"appear as lights"** in the midst of this darkened age (Phil. 2:15). Indeed, Jesus assures us that, when we embrace undistracted devotion toward God, our **"whole body also is full of light"** (Luke 11:34 KJV).

Unfortunately, we have also relied greatly on the strength and ideas of man. We have had light, but it has been dimmed by our worldliness. We have had power, but it has been minimized by our unbelief. The fact is, while we have been created for God's glory, our traditions of unbelief and worldliness have cast upon us their shadow. We can receive much more light and power than we have allowed ourselves.

As we enter the last hours of this age, the Lord will come to us as a refiner's fire and fuller's soap (see Mal. 3:1–4). During this time, His purpose is to wash **"away the filth of the daughters of Zion . . . by the spirit of judgment and the spirit of burning"** (Isa. 4:4).[1]

I do you no service by telling you this cleansing will be easy; it will not. Paul warns, this day shall be **"revealed with fire; and the fire itself will test the quality of each man's work"** (1 Cor. 3:13). The judgments and purges of

God will be deep, and not all who call themselves Christians will submit to them. Yet, for those who embrace the fire of God, the fire itself will become the source of glory in their lives:

> **Then the Lord will create over the whole area of Mount Zion and over her assemblies a cloud by day, even smoke, and the brightness of a flaming fire by night; for over all the glory will be a canopy.** —Isaiah 4:5

God's glory will become a shelter for those He purifies. Because we are sons and daughters of light, the day of the Lord shall not come to us like a thief, but as an answer to our prayers and fulfillment to our longing. Indeed, as sons of light, we shall herald the greater light of His return.

THE DAWN

The day of the Lord, like the dawning of any calendar day, does not burst forth abruptly. It is not pitch black at 5:59 A.M. and then, suddenly, bright morning the next minute. The night sky gradually recedes, retreating from the approaching rays of light. Even before the sun breaks, the morning star faithfully heralds the coming dawn, announcing to the world still in darkness that light is at hand.

The morning star, which is actually the planet Venus, is situated in our sky just above the eastern horizon. It is in such a place as to reflect the light of the sun before the sunrise. The light of the morning star is a very small, but beautiful, preview of the coming day.

The picture of the morning star serves well the prophetic image of the church at the end of the age. Concerning the end times, Peter wrote:

And so we have the prophetic word made more sure, to which you do well to pay attention as to a lamp shining in a dark place, until the day dawns and the morning star arises in your hearts. —2 Peter 1:19

The ancients were fully aware that the morning star appeared while it was still night. Here, Peter is saying that *before* the day of the Lord breaks, the morning star shall rise in our hearts!

We generate no light ourselves. It is only our position at the end of the age that enables us to reflect the day that is coming—all the glory belongs to Jesus! He Himself is the **"bright morning star"** (Rev. 22:16).

This unveiling of Christ rising in His people, like the morning star before dawn, is perfectly consistent with what we read earlier from Isaiah: **"Arise, shine; for your light has come, and the glory of the Lord has risen upon you"** (Isa. 60:1).

When will the glory rise? Just as the morning star rises while it is still night, so the glory of God shall rise within us when **"darkness will cover the earth, and deep darkness the peoples"** (v. 2).

Even as you read these words, the glory of the age to come, **"which is Christ in you, the hope of glory"** (Col. 1:27) already resides in your spirit. Ours is an inheritance of glory, given to us by Jesus the night before He died. He said, **"And the glory which Thou hast given Me I have given to them; that they may be one, just as We are one; I in them, and Thou in Me, that they may be perfected in unity"** (John 17:22–23).

This gift of Christ's glory is the source and essence of true spiritual harmony. Our unity is not the offspring of compromise; it is the consequence of Christ's Presence. It is His glory which produces our unity, in turn causing the world to believe (see John 17:21).

Just for a moment, forget about the increasing darkness in the world around you. Look at the prayer, unity, reconciliation, and renewal movements that have been increasing in the church in recent years. While darkness has covered the earth, the Morning Star of Christ's actual Presence has already begun to rise in His people!

He is the One who has been invisibly, yet powerfully, bringing the church together. He is washing us with the water of His Word, cleansing our divisions and prayerlessness. He is not only preparing us for the harvest, *He is preparing us for His glory.* As a herald of the day of the Lord, the Morning Star of His Presence is, even now, rising in our hearts!

9

THE SIGN

The greatest sign of the end will be the ever-expanding, victorious Presence of the Lord Jesus. If we follow His Presence, we shall be filled with His glory.

THE "PAROUSIA"

When the Lord spoke of His second coming, He used several distinct yet interrelated words. One of the most commonly used words, *erchomai,* clearly meant "to come" or "an arrival." However, there was another word which was also translated "coming." That word was *Parousia.* It actually meant "a being alongside" or "presence" (see Young's concordance under *coming,* or Strong's concordance #3952).

In the original Greek language of the Scriptures, these words *erchomai* (coming) and *Parousia* (presence), though similar in meaning, were not interchangeable. According to *Vine's Expository Dictionary of New Testament Words*, the Parousia actually spanned the entire time frame of Christ's interaction with the world at the end of the age (see pages 208–209).[1]

Yet, Jesus reveals certain things that, in my opinion, imply the Parousia will last longer than just the seven years traditionally ascribed to this period. After listing all the signs of the end times in Mark 13, Jesus concludes: **"Even so, you too, when you see these things happening, recognize that He is near, right at the door"** (Mark 13:29). From the *very beginning* of the decades of signs and warnings Jesus says that He will be **"near, right at the door."**

Luke presents this same concept but provides a sense of chronological movement to Jesus' words. In Luke's gospel, He quotes the Lord as saying, **"But when these things begin to take place, straighten up and lift up your heads, because your redemption is drawing near"** (Luke 21:28).

Jesus said that when these things *begin* to take place He will be near. From the *beginning* of the sign period, the Lord affirms a positional **"drawing near"** which will continue until He is literally **"right at the door."**

Like in the vision which I presented in chapter five, Jesus said that the final act of redemption is something that is *physically* drawing near (see also Heb. 10:25; Rom. 13:11–12). These two statements lead me to believe that the entire sign-period is activated directly by Christ's increasing Presence, the Parousia, at the end of the age.

Perhaps there are two stages to this unfolding: The first, an extended period of divine warnings and divine preparation through which the Lord seeks to awaken repentance and spiritual maturity among His people. The second, shorter period traditionally identified as the seven-year-long Parousia, is when the rapture and tribulation occur.

Either way, to know that the *Parousia* actually means "Presence" provides us with a profound insight in understanding where our focus should be both now and throughout the end of the age. Indeed, to know the Lord will increasingly manifest Himself in His Presence *before* He physically returns is to hear the whisper of God's truth as He leads us to the fountain of His glory.

A STRANGE QUESTION

Matthew, chapter 24, is perhaps the most frequently quoted text in the Bible regarding end time events. The disciples asked the Lord, **"Tell us, when will these things be, and what will be the sign of Your coming, and of the end of the age?"** (Matt. 24:3).

In His answer, Jesus unveiled the prophetic highlights of two events: the destruction of the temple and the conditions in the world at the end of the age. The first event would occur within the disciples' lifetime; the second half of His answer, I believe, is being fulfilled in our days.

The question seems plain enough on the surface, but a deeper look provokes an investigation. *What was really in their minds when they asked Jesus about the sign of His coming?* Up to this moment, the disciples had not accepted or understood that Jesus was leaving. Thus, it seems unlikely they would so casually query Him about His return.

Remember, this conversation occurred before the Last Supper. Only then did Jesus finally convince His disciples that He was returning to the Father (see John 13–17). Up to this point, they may have heard Christ's words about His death, but the reality of His departure never once registered.

Also, and this is just as important: *The disciples had no knowledge of the rapture.* If we study the gospels, prior to this conversation there had been no mention of the gathering together of the saints in any of Jesus' teachings. The first time the Lord touches on the rapture, and that quite briefly, is at the end of His response to their question (Matt. 24:31).

What, then, were the disciples really thinking when they asked about Christ's coming? For if they had never grasped that He was leaving, and they were ignorant of the rapture, why were they asking about His return?

THE SIGN OF HIS PRESENCE

If we look at their question from a different angle, perhaps we will gain insight into their inquiry. In their question, the word translated as "coming" is *Parousia,* "Presence." Dr. Robert Young, the respected compiler of *Young's Analytical Concordance,* also produced his own interpretation of the Scriptures. In his version, called *Young's Literal Translation of the Holy Bible,* the disciple's question is rendered as follows: **"Tell us, when shall these be? And what is the sign of thy Presence, and of the full end of the age?"** (Matt. 24:3)

Young's translation implies that the apostles were asking for more than the calendar day of Christ's actual return. In essence, they were asking, "What is the sign of Your *Presence* which will consummate the full end of the age?"

We would all agree that there is a difference between the calendar day of Christ's return and the season of spiritual fulness introducing it. As I understand Scripture, when Jesus actually returns, the heavens will roll up like a scroll and the earth will shake and totter. The Lord will emerge from eternity and visibly appear in our world; His glory, so bright and expansive, will obscure even the light of the sun. Every eye will see Him: beautiful and terrible, glorified and sovereign, accompanied by innumerable angels and the resurrected dead in Christ. Who will need a "sign" to confirm that this really is Christ coming in glory from the heavens? It seems logical to me that if the disciples did not know about the rapture, neither were they asking about it.

However, from a number of Jesus' teachings concerning His kingdom, the disciples clearly were anticipating a time when Christ's kingdom would emerge in a worldwide display of glory and power. John the Baptist and Jesus both proclaimed the nearness of the kingdom of heaven. Indeed, the disciples were taught to pray for the kingdom to come on earth, and Jesus promised that **"some** [of His disciples] **shall not taste death until they see the kingdom of God after it has come with power"** (Mark 9:1).

When the disciples asked about the arrival of Christ's Presence, I believe it was regarding this expected time of the kingdom. Indeed, this was not a new revelation, but one found in many places in the Old Testament. Daniel foretold a time when, **"in the days"** of the last civilizations on earth, **"the God of heaven will set up a kingdom which will never be destroyed."** He continued that this kingdom would **"crush and put an end to all [other] kingdoms, but it will itself endure forever"** (Dan. 2:44; see also Dan. 7:18, 22).

The eschatology for the *kingdom* had plenty of support from both Jesus' teaching and the Old Testament prophets. This view of God's kingdom coming with power is not "kingdom now" or "dominion" theology; the whole world will not be subdued by Christians "so that" Jesus can return. However, the disciples certainly expected a unique time when Christ's expansive Presence would be revealed, a dispensational time when **"the kingdom of God . . . has come with power"** (Mark 9:1).

TIME TO SHINE

When the disciples asked, **"What is the sign of thy Presence,"** they were expecting an outpouring of the Lord's glory and power. This they identified as His kingdom, which they believed would come in fulness during their lifetime. Remember, I am not saying this time of Christ's

Presence will take the place of the rapture; only that it will precede it.

A simple glance through a concordance reveals that the gospels index over 110 references to the kingdom of God; Jesus mentions the word *church* only three times. The early disciples considered themselves **"sons of the kingdom"** (Matt. 13:38).

To participate in the time of glory was the compelling motive in the lives of Jesus' followers. Of course, they viewed the kingdom of God as a realm they were currently in, but they knew it would expand into worldwide fulfillment (Mark 1:15; Matt. 13:31–32; 36–43).

Jesus explained that the kingdom would undergo a period of defilement, where tares and wheat grew together (Matt. 13:41–42). However, a final cleansing would occur during the last years of the age. With no mention yet of the rapture, Jesus told His disciples to expect a time when the **"righteous will shine forth as the sun in the kingdom of their Father"** (Matt. 13:43).

James and John articulated the desire of all the disciples when they asked, **"Grant that we may sit in Your glory, one on Your right, and one on Your left"** (Mark 10:37). They all knew the glory was coming; who would possess the biggest share was what filled their minds. Could it be that this shining **"forth as the sun"** and sitting in the Lord's glory is what the disciples anticipated during the Parousia?

THEY SAW THE DAY OF GLORY

Consider: The disciples who asked Jesus about the time of the end were Peter, James, John, and Andrew (Mark 13:3). The first three had been with Jesus on the Mount of Transfiguration when the Lord **"shone like the sun"** (Matt. 17:2).

Immediately prior to the Transfiguration, Jesus told His disciples, **"Truly I say to you, there are some of those who are standing here who shall not taste death until they see the kingdom of God after it has come with power"** (Mark 9:1).

Jesus plainly stated that some of His disciples would see the **"kingdom of God after it has come with power."** The very next verse connects what Jesus just said with the Transfiguration: **"And six days later, Jesus took with Him Peter and James and John, and brought them up to a high mountain by themselves. And He was transfigured before them"** (Mark 9:2).

Jesus truly showed "some" of His disciples what the kingdom of God would look like in the day of power. This is significant: *The disciples who questioned Jesus concerning the sign of His Presence are those who were with Him on the Mount of Transfiguration!*

Let me point out that, in the rapture, we shall be changed from earthly bodies to heavenly bodies. At that time, Paul tells us, we will put on a nature that is similar to Christ's (see Phil. 3:21). John, who was with Jesus during the Transfiguration, tells us that **"it has not appeared as yet what we shall be"** (1 John 3:2). On the Mount of Transfiguration, Jesus revealed the day of power and glory that *precedes* the rapture. During the rapture, our mortal bodies will put on immortality. But on the Mount of Transfiguration, though filled with glory, Jesus still had a body that could suffer and die.

Peter was so overwhelmed by the unveiling of the coming glory that at the end of his life this vision was still the compelling experience of his life (2 Peter 1:14)! Yet, Peter was not looking back on this incident; he was looking forward to having it happen to himself! He wrote:

> **For we did not follow cleverly devised tales when we made known to you the power and coming of our Lord Jesus Christ, but we were eyewitnesses of His majesty.**
>
> **For when He received honor and glory from God the Father, such an utterance as this was made to Him by the Majestic Glory, "This is My beloved Son with whom I am well-pleased" —and we ourselves heard this utterance made from heaven when we were with Him on the holy mountain.**   —2 Peter 1:16–18

When Peter speaks of the **"power and coming"** of our Lord, the word translated "coming" is *Parousia,* "Presence." Young's literal translation reads, **"we did make known to you the power and Presence of our Lord Jesus Christ."** Peter was referring to his time with Christ **"on the holy mountain."** Here, in this experience with Christ in glory, the disciples came to expect a future breakthrough that far exceeded their experience in the kingdom to date.

THE LORD IS PREPARING US FOR GLORY

As a result of the Lord's chastening, we have seen many breakthroughs in the church: the emergence and momentum of the prayer movement, and the cleansing of divisions between denominations and races. The church is experiencing revival and renewal in a number of places. At the source of these holy and significant changes is the increasing Presence of the Lord Jesus Christ. I believe God is working in the church to create the necessary conditions for an awesome baptism of glory.

In the following chapters we will reach for God's grace as the Lord comes to liberate us for this hour and upgrade our lives to kingdom standards. Yet, let me conclude with one more text. This was Paul's prayer for the church in the first century; it is my prayer for the church today.

> **[That you may really come] to know—practically, through experience for yourselves—the love of Christ, which far surpasses mere knowledge (without experience); that you may be filled (through all your being) unto all the fullness of God—[that is] may have the richest measure of the divine Presence, and become a body wholly filled and flooded with God Himself!** —Ephesians 3:19 AMPLIFIED

Our calling is **"unto all the fullness of God."** What awaits us *before* the rapture is nothing less than the **"richest measure of the divine Presence."** This, indeed, is what the "Days of His Presence" shall reveal: a people **"wholly filled and flooded with God Himself!"**

Part Three

RISE AND WALK

"I have seen his ways, but I will heal him;
I will lead him and restore comfort to him
    and to his mourners,
creating the praise of the lips.
Peace, peace to him who is far
    and to him who is near," says the Lord,
    "and I will heal him."
                            —Isaiah 57:18–19

10

FREEDOM
TO PRISONERS

During the last hours of this age a great army shall arise; it shall consist of the lame and the oppressed. Though they have been last, many will become first to enter His glory.

When we consider the waning hours of this age—the times of judgment, glory, and terror—we must keep our eyes upon the grace and purposes of God. The Scriptures tell us that Jesus Christ is the same yesterday, today, and forever (see Heb. 13:8). The person we read about in the Gospels is eternally the same Redeemer, seated at the right hand of God in the heavens.

We may wonder, *Isn't He coming with great wrath?* Yes. But the One worthy to open the seals of judgment, though He is the Lion of Judah, is also a **"Lamb standing, as if slain"** (Rev. 5:6). Even in the day of His wrath, God's hand is ever guided by His redemptive mercy. Many who have failed the Lord during these past years will discover He is coming to set us free from the burden of defeat and condemnation.

Indeed, when Jesus began His ministry, He opened the book of the prophet Isaiah to where it was written concerning His mission. **"The Spirit of the Lord God is upon me,"** He said, **"Because the Lord has anointed me to bring good news to the afflicted; He has sent me to bind up the brokenhearted, to proclaim liberty to captives, and freedom to prisoners; to proclaim the favorable year of the Lord"** (Isa. 61:1–2). He then closed the book and said, **"Today this Scripture has been fulfilled in your hearing"** (Luke 4:21).

What is striking here is that Jesus ended this prophecy about Himself in the middle of a sentence. Isaiah's promise continues as it describes the complete purpose of God in Christ. It reads, **"To proclaim the favorable year of the Lord, and the day of vengeance of our God"** (Isa. 61:2).

The Lord's mercy always triumphs over judgment (James 2:13). God has a **"favorable *year*"** and a **"*day* of vengeance."** Over 1,900 years separate the two parts of this prophecy.

Even so, when we think of vengeance, our imaginations often rush ahead to hailstones, earthquakes, and calamities; we hope that we will be nowhere near when God's judgments fall. Yet, one primary manifestation of God's wrath against those who are profane is that He pours out His mercy and deliverance upon those who seek to be holy! From the point of view of the righteous, what happens during the **"day of vengeance of our God"** is wonderful! He comes:

> **To comfort all who mourn, to grant those who mourn in Zion, giving them a garland instead of ashes, the oil of gladness instead of mourning, the mantle of praise instead of a spirit of fainting. So they will be called oaks of righteousness,**

the planting of the Lord, that He may be glorified. —Isaiah 61:2–3

One very significant aspect of God's wrath is to destroy that which has been oppressing His people! Many Christians fight with evil spirits. Isaiah refers to one such enemy as the **"spirit of fainting"** (KJV reads **"heaviness"**). Other demons rob us of joy, strength, and health. Against these the Lord has a day of reckoning. As God judges these spirits, we obtain **"comfort"** for our mourning, a **"garland"** for ashes, and **"gladness"** for sorrow. The Lord gives us a mantle of praise and thanksgiving instead of the weariness and heaviness that so often burden the righteous in their war against evil.

The Lord's goal is to liberate us, but not so we can relax under our fig tree! He frees us so we can free others. He says, **"Then they will rebuild the ancient ruins, they will raise up the former devastations, and they will repair the ruined cities, the desolations of many generations"** (Isa. 61:4).

Many who today are **"former devastations"** shall be raised up to serve God in gladness at the end of the age! Drunkards and drug addicts shall become some of the most effective servants of God; many gang members and homosexuals will pass through the regenerating work of the Holy Spirit and, as new creatures in Christ, be used mightily by God in the days ahead.

Many others who are convinced the Lord has rejected them will find God's grace extended powerfully toward their hearts. The first evil Christ will judge and remove is the burden of hopelessness. Even to each of us today, the Lord still comes **"to bind up the brokenhearted, to proclaim liberty to captives, and freedom to prisoners."**

11

DOOR OF HOPE

Faith is the substance of the things hoped for.
Without a living hope in God, our faith is meaningless.
The first stage of deliverance is the restoration of hope.

The Lord was about to prosper Israel with the wealth of the Canaanites, but only if the spoils of their first battle at Jericho were completely dedicated to God. One man, Achan, defied the Lord's edict and took silver, gold, and a garment from Shinar, and then hid the spoils in his tent. As a result of his sin, thirty-six Israelites died in their next battle—defeated and humiliated by the tiny city of Ai.

After the Lord exposed Achan as the perpetrator, Joshua took him, along with his family and possessions, and brought them all to a valley. There, Israel's leader said, **"'Why have you troubled us? The Lord will trouble you this day.' And all Israel stoned them with stones; . . . Therefore the name of that place has been called the valley of Achor to this day"** (Josh. 7:25–26).

The word *Achor* meant "troubling." It represented the trouble and pain caused by one to others. Certainly, the most terrible thing Achan experienced was that his sin caused his wife and children to die with him. As they huddled together awaiting this horrible judgment, the guilt and regret flooding Achan's mind must have been insufferable.

PERSONAL FAILURE

In time, the valley of Achor came to symbolize the worst of punishments. It was a place of death and desolation. Today, of course, we do not stone those whose sin or irresponsibility has caused others grief. Still, sin has consequences, and though we may not be physically stoned for our failure, the effects of public condemnation can be just as crushing to the human spirit. The fact is, too many of us have known a personal valley of Achor, where our moral negligence or ill-advised actions caused another's suffering.

Perhaps you committed adultery and your spouse and children are devastated. It might be that your anxious or careless driving caused an accident, resulting in great suffering, or possibly even another person's death. Or maybe your lack of Christian example has caused your children to turn from God. The possible ways of falling are endless, but the result is nearly always the same: it is as though a curse rests on your life.

Not only does your own heart condemn you, you have been convinced by the words and attitudes of others that you deserve your present misery. Public censure has the same effect on your spirit as Achan's stoning had on his flesh, only what died in you was hope. Where once you could look with anticipation toward the future, now heartache and regret block your view.

Only virtue, made pure and strong by true repentance, can displace the burden of self-condemnation. Thus, the only correct response to wrong actions and their consequences is the transforming work of the Holy Spirit. Unfortunately, the enemy has many Christians trapped in unbelief and self-condemnation. They know what they did was wrong and they hate it, but they cannot unburden themselves of the guilt.

Remember, in the previous chapter we read that our Redeemer came to proclaim liberty to those who are "prisoners." Is He speaking only of those who are incarcerated in jails? No, His mission is for all of us who are prisoners of their past. *God wants us to learn from our failures, not be held captive to them.* He came to deliver and restore those whose dreams lie buried in the valley of Achor.

PERSONAL TRAGEDY

The burdens we carry may have nothing to do with moral failure. They might have come from any number of life's calamities.

One of the worst ordeals for the soul is the death of a loved one. Such a loss can leave us excessively burdened and trapped in the past. The story of Abraham's father, Terah, gives us an insightful picture of a man who could not depart from the loss of a loved one.

Terah had three sons: Abram, Nahor, and Haran. The Bible tells us, **"Haran died in the presence of his father"** (Gen. 11:28). To lose your son can produce terrible heartache; to have him die in your arms can be utterly devastating.

In time, Terah took his family and left Ur of the Chaldeans in search of a new destiny in Canaan. En route, however, Terah had to pass through a city with the same name as his deceased son, Haran. Instead of continuing on to Canaan, the Scripture says Terah **"went as far as Haran, and settled there"** (v. 31).

Longing for a deceased loved one is normal. However, life's tragedies also have a way of obligating us to a false loyalty which prohibits the release of our pain. Without notice, a face in an airport or a song on the radio unlocks our hearts and, suddenly, we are enveloped in sorrow. How quickly we re-enter the place of our grief; how easy it is to settle there!

"And Terah died in Haran" (v. 32). Not only did Terah settle in Haran, he died there. The wording is both prophetic and significant. Perhaps it was a false sense of guilt that held him hostage: *If only I had done such and such, my son would not have died!* Whatever the reason, Terah was never able to live beyond Haran's death.

We must also see that, as painful as the loss of a loved one is, we cannot permit the wounds of our past to nullify what God has for us in our future. Even if we enter limping, we must not settle for something outside our destiny. God's grace is here now. With His help, we must *choose* to journey on to Canaan, or we, too, will die in Haran.

A TIME FOR HEALING

These two things, personal failure and personal tragedy, can place cruel burdens of oppression and guilt upon our souls. God's response to our need is that, in addition to forgiving our sins, He has laid on Christ **"the guilt of us all"** (Isa. 53:6 NAB). Whether our guilt is justified or not, it must be lifted from our shoulders and placed on Christ.

Today, a renewal is occurring in various parts of the world; God is restoring *joy* to His people. Many whom the Lord has touched were weighed down—just like you might be—with either moral failure or tragedy. In the very place where our deferred hopes produced heart sickness (Prov. 13:12), now Christ has come **"to bind up the broken-hearted"** (Isa. 61:1). Where once sorrow and heaviness reigned, He gives a **"garland instead of ashes, the oil of gladness instead of mourning, the mantle of praise instead of a spirit of fainting"** (Isa. 61:3).

No longer will church attendance be a penance for your failures. From now on you shall enter His gates with thanksgiving. Indeed, to every Christian struggling with an unbearable burden, the Lord says, *You are still My bride.*

Indeed, speaking of this very valley of troubling, the Lord has promised:

> **I will allure her, bring her into the wilderness, and speak kindly to her. Then I will give her her vineyards from there, and the valley of Achor as a door of hope. And she will sing there as in the days of her youth.** —Hosea 2:14–15

The fruitfulness of God's blessing, from this day forward, shall increase in your life. And there in **"the valley of Achor,"** the scene of your deepest wounds or worst failures, the Lord has placed for you a **"door of hope."** His goal is nothing less than to restore to you the song of the Lord, that you might sing again **"as in the days of [your] youth."**

12

TO WALK
WITH GOD

In the days ahead many will be stirred by proclamations, both true and false, of ominous events set for fulfillment on specific dates. However, we are not being prepared for a "date" but for a marriage. It is the depth of our day-by-day relationship with Christ that defines walking with God at the end of the age.

The confidence we have as we face tomorrow is rooted in the quality of our walk with God today. Thus, as these days unfold, the way of the Lord will be revealed for what it truly is: *a narrow path upon which we walk with God.* It is an indisputable truth: the only way to prepare for Jesus' second coming is to faithfully obey what He commanded in His *first* coming—and His first command was **"Follow Me"** (John 1:43).

What does it mean to "follow" Jesus but that we walk faithfully with Him throughout our life. The fact is, we anticipate the nearness of the Lord, but we do not know when He might return. While I believe we are very near to the end of the age, still it may be many years before some of the unfulfilled prophecies come to pass. Regardless, our call is to follow the Lamb—to walk with Him every day.

If we study the Scriptures, we will see that, from the beginning, the Lord always provided for those who walked with Him in His Presence. No matter what occurred in the world, God's servants were not held hostage to the fears and anxieties of their times. Their walk with God prepared them for all things.

Jesus said the days prior to His return would be as the days of Noah. Let us look again at Noah's life. God did not give Noah a predetermined date specifying when the flood would come. The Lord gave Noah two things: a *task*, which was to build the ark, and *time* to get the job done.

The Almighty could have destroyed wickedness in a heartbeat. Yet, the Scriptures tell us that the **"patience of God kept waiting . . . during the construction of the ark"** (1 Peter 3:20). The priority of God was focused not on what was to be destroyed but on what was being built.

Too many of us are so focused on what the devil is doing that we fail to see what God is doing. *The focus of the Lord is not on how dark evil becomes but how Christlike the church becomes!* There is a grace streaming from God's heart. In the midst of great darkness, the Lord has purposed to bring glory to Himself and protection to His people.

God told Noah to build the ark. When the task was completed, then the flood came. We also have a task, a vision from God: *build the House of the Lord and participate in the harvest of the nations.* Jesus did not say, "When evil gets worse the harvest begins." He said, **"when the crop permits . . . the harvest has come"** (Mark 4:29).

Certainly, God's highest plans will not be diverted by the increase of wickedness. One may say that God's justice demands He destroy the wicked! Yes, but His *nature* demands His *good* plans and promises concerning His glory in the church first be fulfilled!

Look again at Noah. Noah lived at a time when **"every intent of the thoughts of his** [man's] **heart was only evil continually."** His world, like ours, **"was corrupt in the sight of God, and . . . filled with violence"** (Gen. 6:5, 11).

Yet, during these same days, **"Noah found favor in the eyes of the Lord"** (Gen. 6:8). What was unique about Noah? How did he find the preserving grace of God in his life? The Scriptures tell us, **"Noah was a righteous man, blameless in his time; Noah walked with God"** (Gen. 6:9).

I love this Scripture: *Noah walked with God.* What does it mean to walk with God? It means that we stay yielded to His Word and attentive to His Presence. Though we do not see Him, we know Him. We have found our place of security in the Almighty. Our peace comes from Him, not people, places, or things.

The name *Noah* means "rest." As the Lord's servant, Noah not only knew his mission in life, but he found His place of rest in God alone. Step-by-step, day-by-day, Noah lived in the Lord's Presence. Noah walked with God and was intimate with Him.

But to know someone deeply does not happen quickly. It takes time to penetrate through the veil of unknowing into the place of enduring friendship and intimacy. This is why *walking* with God is so pleasing to Him, for it creates a time-tested relationship between God and man. We no longer are controlled by the opinions, criticisms, and approval of the world around us. Only as our walk with God matures does intimacy with the Creator truly begin and peace about the future increase.

Consider Abraham. Abraham was called the friend of God (see Isa. 41:8). When he was ninety-nine years old, the Lord appeared to him and said, **"I am God Almighty; walk before Me, and be blameless"** (Gen. 17:1). Walking with

God leads to purity and intimate friendship with God. It is the source of becoming blameless.

Abraham's descendants, Isaac and Jacob, also walked with God (Gen. 48:15). The lifelong companionship between the Almighty and these patriarchs set the standard for all who followed, from the kings and the prophets of Israel to each Christian who walks with God today.

MY OWN EXPERIENCE

We should not be hard on those who have falsely affixed a prophetic event or even the Second Coming to a specific date. It is usually the sincerity of these people that propels their prophecies into regional or national prominence. I, myself, was swept up in a similar experience in the mid-seventies.

Those were days when threats of nuclear war seemed everywhere; many Christians were predicting divine judgment for America. During those days, I came across an article about a huge comet that was due to appear on Christmas Day, 1975. Previously unknown, the comet was named *Kohoutek* after the Hungarian astronomer who discovered it. The signs of the times confirmed my fears, but when I read in a religious publication that *Kohoutek* meant "the wolf that devours the lamb," I felt certain that this was a "sign in the heavens" confirming that the end was near.

Compelled by my inner convictions, I began to warn every church in Detroit, all 1,200 of them, that the world would end that Christmas. I even managed to become a guest on the most-watched morning talk show in Detroit, where I warned as many as three million people of God's imminent wrath.

Christmas came and went and nothing happened. The comet was an over-exaggerated astronomical flop. I had been so sure of my insights, so fearfully compelled by the signs of the times, yet so wrongly informed. Then in late

January, I happened to meet a woman fluent in Hungarian. I asked her to translate *Kohoutek* into English. She thought it meant something like "add a tomato to the stew."

God knew my motives were right, even though my knowledge was wrong. Out of that humiliating experience I began to research other "end of the world" movements in church history. In my study, I discovered two significant items that occurred in Europe. Masses of people were convinced the year 1666 would see the rise of the antichrist. This thought led to waves of fanaticism and fear which spread from country to country.

I had also been reading a devotional containing a series of letters written by a man named Brother Lawrence, a monk who served Christ as a dishwasher in a monastery. The simple, yet profound, sense of God's Presence that accompanied Brother Lawrence made this book, *The Practice of the Presence of God,* an enduring Christian classic. But what changed my life was that his first letters were written in the year *1666,* during the time when Europe was awash with fear of the antichrist! For all the turmoil in the world around him, at least one soul dwelt in the peace of Jesus Christ.

Brother Lawrence serves as a model for our generation. For when the terrors and confusion of the end of the age increase, it is only in the Lord's Presence that we shall find a calm harbor. And to truly know Him *then,* we must walk with Him *now.*

ENOCH WALKED WITH GOD

One of my favorite texts is from Genesis 5:22–24. It reads, **"Then Enoch walked with God three hundred years . . . and he was not, for God took him."** Hebrews 11:5 tells us that Enoch had **"obtained the witness . . . he was pleasing to God."**

Enoch walked with God *300 years.* Every day, Enoch arose and sought the Lord, walking faithfully with the Almighty. Eventually, Enoch became so pleasing to God that, without passing through death, He was taken home to be with the Lord.

So also with us, when we faithfully walk with God we bring great pleasure to our Father. The Scripture says that Enoch **"obtained the witness"** that his life was **"pleasing to God."** God communicated His pleasure to Enoch. To know the pleasure of God is to taste the nectar of heaven itself.

Whatever may happen in the future, the God of the future is walking with us today. And while we may not be able to see into tomorrow, our faithfulness to Christ today is our best security for whatever lies ahead.

As the first person raptured by Christ, Enoch sets the standard for all whom Jesus will one day gather to Himself. They simply and passionately walk with God.

Part Four

FROM VISITATION TO HABITATION

A voice is calling,
"Clear the way for the Lord in the wilderness;
make smooth in the desert a highway for our God.

"Let every valley be lifted up,
And every mountain and hill be made low;
And let the rough ground become a plain,
And the rugged terrain a broad valley;

"Then the glory of the Lord will be revealed,
And all flesh will see it together;
For the mouth of the Lord has spoken."
                                    —Isaiah 40:3–5

13

IN A TIME
OF VISITATION

God does not deliver us for our sakes, but for His. He frees us so we can fulfill His purpose.

There had not been a prophet in Israel for more than 400 years. Now, in the spirit and power of Elijah, John the Baptist stood in the Judean wilderness. Lightning flashed from his eyes as his message thundered across the terrain of Judea; it shook the landscape of Israel's soul. The storm of God had returned.

Historians tell us that John's penetrating ministry brought nearly one million people to a baptism of repentance. It was an unprecedented beginning to a time of visitation.

Into this electrified atmosphere of awakened faith Jesus came, bringing miracles previously unseen in Israel's history. The Presence of the living God had come through Christ; the kingdom of heaven was at hand.

Yet, after three years of what seemed like revival and signs and wonders, Jesus lamented over the nation. He wept at the shallowness of the people and their failure to **"recognize the time of** [their] **visitation"** (Luke 19:44).

In what way did they miss this visitation of God? Hundreds of thousands responded to John's call for repentance. Clearly, people were awed by the supernatural: The incurable were cured; the demoniacs, delivered. And what of the multitudes who followed Jesus into the wilderness—the ones who ate the loaves and fish? Did not they, at least, recognize the uniqueness of this hour?

Obviously, the throngs were quite familiar with one aspect of visitation: that which relieves the burden of the afflicted (see Luke 4:18–19). Yet, the goal of God in visitation is not just that man in his sorrows is made happy but that man in his rebellion is made obedient.

God had set His focus on Israel so that Israel, with burdens relieved, could set their focus on God. Indeed, in the Bible, the word *visitation* also refers to a time of being inspected and examined closely. In other words, *God is looking for something to arise during a time of visitation.*

For the most part, Israel failed to recognize what God was after in healing, delivering, and restoring the multitudes. The consequences of failing to discern God's expectations are very serious.

Seeing the repercussions of Israel's disobedience, Jesus wept. He said,

> **For the days shall come upon you when your enemies will throw up a bank before you, and surround you, and hem you in on every side, and will level you to the ground and your children within you, . . . because you did not recognize the time of your visitation.** —Luke 19:43–44

What the Lord seeks goes beyond the immediate comfort of His people. In fact, as He gives us greater liberty, He expects greater obedience. At the very same moment that God removes our burdens, He removes our excuses as well.

The Lord does not free us so we can return to the type of behavior that caused our misery in the first place! Even as you are being blessed, refreshed, and healed, remember: **"from everyone who has been given much shall much be required"** (Luke 12:48).

THE DIVINE OBJECTIVE

What does God expect from His time of visitation? He looks to unite His people, creating within them a permanent dwelling place for Himself. He cleans and heals us so He can unveil His glory through us. Thus, reconciliation and oneness with God culminates in reconciliation and oneness with each other!

We plainly see Christ's heartache in Luke 13. Looking at Israel's capital city, the Messiah cried out, **"O Jerusalem, Jerusalem . . . How often I wanted to gather your children together, just as a hen gathers her brood under her wings, and you would not have it!"** (Luke 13:34) Jesus sought *many times* to unite His people but they **"would not have it."** Unyielding, they accepted His blessings but not His Lordship.

You see, God is after something in blessing us. He is not an eternal "Santa Claus" whose only joy is in giving us gifts. If God has blessed you, it is so you can bless others. If He has forgiven your debts, it is so you might forgive what is owed to you. If He has joined you to Himself, it is so He can unite you with others in His body.

THE BEGINNING OF VISITATION

I believe the church is in a new time of divine visitation. Over the past several years, the Lord has raised up an armada of intercessory ministries around the world. Through their efforts, multitudes have come together in citywide prayer, solemn assemblies, prayer summits, and reconciliation services. God has used the earnestness of this intercession to bring millions to repentance. The prayer movement has touched the heart of God; in turn, He has touched the heart of man.

As a result of this prayer movement, the church is seeing the beginning of visitation throughout the world. Renewal, revival, and supernatural manifestations are being reported almost daily. Many feel we are closer to a great awakening than at any other time in this century.

Yet, a holy fear grips my heart. *When we cry for God to visit us, do we really know what we are asking?* When we entreat the Almighty for His kingdom, are we ready to surrender ours? The same prayer that asks for His unrestrained blessing also calls for His corrective judgments on our disobedience. We are asking for God *to be God* in our midst!

Most of first-century Israel misunderstood the long-term goal of visitation, and they ultimately suffered greatly for it. Nevertheless, on Pentecost, Christ's disciples carried the visitation of God into its eternal purpose: They became His dwelling place.

This was the Lord's ultimate goal for His disciples: that they would find oneness with Himself and with one another. Consider: He gave us His Word not just to edify us, but **"that [we] may all be one"** (John 17:20–21). He gave us His name, not just for our letterheads but, again, that we **"may be one"** (John 17:11). And He gave us His glory for this same reason: that we **"may be one,"** just as He and the Father are One (John 17:22–23). Christ's gift to us is His Word, His name, and His glory; His purpose is that we become one with Him and each other.

The disciples exemplified this fulfillment. They were united in daily prayer (see Acts 3:1). Their intimacy with

God was not born of desperation but devotion. Miracles were ordinary in the extraordinary Presence of Christ.

Knowing their gifts would go to the needy, with great joy people often laid all they owned at the apostles' feet. Truthfully, Peter could say, **"I do not possess silver and gold"** (Acts 3:6). What they possessed was the wealth of the kingdom. In their power, love, and giving they manifested a life of oneness with Christ and with one another: this is the full purpose of God in visitation.

Let us, therefore, recognize that the long-term intention of God is not only to eliminate the pains in our bodies but also to establish His reign in our hearts. Yes, let us continue to pray for revival and to rejoice when we see it. But, with sobriety, let us also remember: In the days of His Presence, the goal of God's visitation is to make us His habitation.

14

RISING TO THE
STATURE OF CHRIST

*This is what revival and visitation look like: people
filled with Jesus!*

I n Paul's epistle to the Ephesians, He explained the
particulars of our destiny at the end of the age: What
awaits us is nothing short of the fulness of Christ in the
fulness of time!

Let us not disqualify ourselves from our destiny because
of an evil and unbelieving heart. Let us not say there are yet
giants occupying our souls which God cannot defeat. Let us
simply *believe* that what He has promised, He is also able
to perform. For certainly there shall be a fulfillment of that
which was spoken by the Lord.

God has laid out the map, He has charted our course
beforehand. Let us hold to His plan and follow His Word.
In truth, whatever we see in Jesus is what God plans to
reveal in us. The works that He did, He promises we shall
do also; **"and greater works than these"** shall we do

before Jesus returns from the Father (John 14:12). It is this vision of attaining Christlikeness that centers us firmly upon the path to doctrinal purity. Without this vision, we are forever distracted by fads and trends.

Not until we clearly and firmly grasp our God-appointed destiny do we begin to develop in true spiritual maturity. As a result of actually embracing our destiny, **"we are no longer to be children, tossed here and there by waves, and carried about by every wind of doctrine"** (Eph. 4:14).

It's important to note that Paul did not specify whether these winds of doctrine were true or false teachings. Dogma does not have to be false to be misleading. Even a true doctrine with an overly exaggerated emphasis can sidetrack us from Christlikeness.

It is here, where we boast in our doctrines and spiritual gifts, that many of us are led astray. For what compels us forward into new religious activity is not always the leading of God but the desire to be known for something other than knowing Jesus Himself. If we do not see conformity to Christ as central to our future, then what may be guiding us is a **"wind of doctrine."**

In the church today there are a number of doctrines that have grown bigger than their scriptural proportions and tend to obscure our vision of Christlikeness. Spiritual warfare and deliverance have become, for some, doctrinal winds that blow them off course. For others, teachings about personal prosperity or the timing of the rapture have turned into unbalanced precepts that easily distract from the truth that is in Jesus.

Some churches overemphasize the doctrine of speaking in tongues or prophecy. Now, I believe that the gifts of the Spirit are for today, but these too can become winds of doctrine.

Again, we are not talking about false teachings but true beliefs that have become caricatures of the Gospel. Correct and balanced doctrinal understanding is fundamental to our spiritual well-being. *When our energies are absorbed more with a particular doctrine than with attaining the character of Christ, we are being misled.*

In the Ephesians' passage referenced earlier, Paul said that it is only our pursuit of Christlikeness that keeps us from being **"tossed here and there by waves"** (Eph. 4:14). A wave is a spiritual phenomenon that sweeps over a church or a city—a spiritual high tide in which we can be washed and healed. A true spiritual wave can release wonderful joy and bring healing to areas within us otherwise untouched by God.

Yet, if we follow after waves, we must recognize: the tide that comes in with manifestations and blessings also goes out. When the wave has passed, it does not mean God has abandoned us or that His ultimate purpose has changed.

A genuine stirring of God's Spirit, either through a fresh doctrinal understanding or through unique spiritual manifestations, should empower us toward conformity to Christ. The fact is, whether we are in a time of preparation or in the glory of a visitation, whether we are carrying the cross or soaring in resurrection power, our goal is still Christlikeness.

If you are confused about what is happening in the church-at-large or even in your own life, remember, God does not want you tossed by waves or carried by doctrines.

You are not rebellious if you think a certain manifestation is too extreme for you. Neither are you out of order if you wonder whether you or your church are too focused on peripheral doctrines instead of reaching for Christ Himself.

The issue is not whether we follow a doctrine or fall under a wave. The real question is whether we will rise to the stature which belongs to the fulness of Christ.

15

SURRENDER OF
THE VISION-KEEPER

*To walk with God is to walk a path of increasing
surrender and trust. Indeed, the time is at hand when the
Lord Jesus shall confront our tendencies to control Him.
Not only will we know doctrinally that Christ is Lord, but
we will also serve Him as Lord.*

CHURCHES IN TRANSITION

If you find yourself more drawn toward prayer than
promotion, more toward humility than hype, you are being
prepared by the Lord for the glory of God. What He is
working in you is typical of what God is establishing in
thousands of other believers.

However, before the Father ultimately reveals Christ as
Lord over the earth, He will first reveal Him as Lord over
the church. And while we should rejoice, we must also take
heed. For until we are standing face-to-face in glory with
Jesus Himself, we are going to be in transition. To each of
us, Christ's call remains, **"Come, follow Me!"** (Luke 18:22)

If we will walk with Him in obedience, He will take us into the fulness of His Presence.

Still, transitions can be frightening. The uncertainty of those passages between spiritual plateaus can hold us hostage to yesterday's blessings. Let us recall with godly fear that the bronze serpent, which brought healing to Israel in the wilderness, by Hezekiah's day had become an idol which had to be torn down. Our hearts must bow to God alone, for even spiritual gifts when isolated from Christ, the Giver, can become idolatrous.

Therefore, to successfully navigate this season of change, the Lord will require of us a fresh surrender to His Lordship. He will demand that our preconceived ideas and expectations be submitted to Him. For if we are continually telling the Holy Spirit where we expect to go, we neutralize our capacity to hear where He wants to take us.

CHRIST IN US

To better understand the changes God is initiating in the church, we are going to study the life of Mary, Jesus' mother. More than any other woman, God had blessed Mary. She alone was granted the wondrous privilege of giving birth to the Son of God.

While the Lord's promise and purpose with Mary were unparalleled, in two significant ways His promise to us is similar. First, even as Mary received Christ into her physical body, we have received Jesus into our spirits. And secondly, as she birthed Christ, our quest is to see Jesus unfettered from the womb of our religion about Him. Our destiny is not just to carry Christ inside but to reveal the fulness of His glory in this world.

Even now, abiding within our spirits, deeper and more profound than our church doctrines, is the actual Spirit of Christ. The consequence of this union of Christ's Spirit with our spirits expands the original seven creation days into the eighth day. We are new creatures in a new creation (see Gal. 6:15). In this new beginning to God's eternal plan, Jesus Christ is the firstborn of a new race of men (1 Cor. 15:45).

As Jesus was both God and man, so the church is actually the dwelling of Christ in the temple of man. There is not a different Jesus in us than He who dwells in heaven. He is Christ wrapped in glory in heaven; He is Christ wrapped in our human flesh on earth.

Our salvation is nothing less than the Perfect One dwelling in the imperfect ones, the Almighty abiding in the feeble, the All-Sufficient God dwelling among insufficient people. This is the mystery and glory of our salvation: *Christ in His completeness has extended Himself into our lives!*

Crucial to the success of His mission is our receiving these truths with faith, determining that they shall be our *reality,* not just our *theology.* It is here, in this carrying of the actual Presence of Christ within us, that we share with Mary the awe of God's purpose for us.

JESUS IN SUBJECTION

While Joseph was a good man, it was Mary who nurtured Jesus and continued to raise Him after Joseph died. In fact, we shall see that Mary became the matriarch of the family. Uniquely, under her spiritual influence, Jesus matured. It was natural that, over time, Mary would consider herself the "Keeper of the Vision; Guardian of Him Who is to Come," for, in truth, she was.

"And He continued in subjection to them" (Luke 2:51). This is an astonishing thought: Jesus, Lord of heaven, in subjection to a lowly carpenter and his wife. Yet if we think about it, is it not equally astonishing that the rule of Christ in His church is, at least in part, subject to our initiatives? He submits Himself to our schedules and to our service times. He works within the confinements of our weaknesses and temperaments. Yet, we should honestly ask ourselves, is it a voice from heaven or the traditions of earth which determines how long we shall worship Him on Sunday morning?

If the Lord so decided, in an instant He could reveal His majesty and draw trembling surrender from all mankind. However, He restrains Himself, choosing not to intimidate but to inspire our obedience. He has chosen to hide His glory not *from* us but *in* us. And then, in order to perfect our character, He subjects Himself to our initiatives of hunger and faith.

However, the fact that Jesus will *accommodate* and submit Himself to the conditions we offer Him does not mean that He has approved of our limitations upon Him. The standard of the church is not the church; it is Christ. And this is our present dilemma: Just as Jesus subjected Himself to Mary and Joseph and they became, for a time, the "Vision-Keepers," so we have assumed that Christ will continue to exist in "subjection" to us. He will not. For as Jesus arises in His Lordship, to save us He must first deliver us from our efforts to control Him.

A TIME TO LET GO

It is significant that Mary still exercised matriarchal supervision over Jesus even after He was a mature man. At the wedding feast in Cana we find Jesus, His disciples, and Mary, the "Vision-Keeper." **"They have no wine,"** Mary told her son. Jesus answered, **"Woman, what do I have to do with you? My hour has not yet come"** (John 2:3–4). In spite of what Jesus just said, Mary tells the servants, **"Whatever He says to you, do it"** (v. 5). While I am amazed at the fact that the Father worked through Mary's orchestration of this miracle, the fact is, Jesus did not come forth to do the will of His mother but His Father. It was time for Jesus, Mary's son, to begin His ministry as Jesus, God's Son.

A significant and necessary reversal of authority was needed in Mary's relationship with Christ—a change which she had not anticipated. In her mind, her sense of influence was simply a continuation of her God-given responsibility as Vision-Keeper.

The problem of control worsened after the miracle at Cana: **"After this He went down to Capernaum, He and His mother, and His brothers, and His disciples; and there they stayed a few days"** (John 2:12). The verse reads, **"He and His mother"** went to Capernaum. Do you see? Mary, the "Keeper of the Vision," has taken what she thinks is a legitimate position, an earned place of influence, with Christ.

In defense of Mary, she clearly has been with Jesus the longest; she has paid the highest price. More than anyone, she has heard the Word and believed it; her faith has borne Christ Himself! She has magnificently served the purposes of God. Perhaps she had every right to think that Christ could work the miracles as long as she remained a guiding influence. Her continued "mothering" was not evil but natural.

However, God had determined it was time for Jesus to be unfettered from all human influences of control. Jesus would now only do the things He saw His Father do.

This, I believe, is where God is jealously directing us: We are being emptied of our agendas, false expectations, and non-biblical traditions so that Christ alone will be Lord over the church. In the next chapter we will see how the Lord delivered Mary. What we are learning now is that, even though we have served as keepers of the vision, we must now surrender to the Lord of the vision.

16

A SWORD WILL
PIERCE YOUR HEART

The plans of God are full of surprises.

No matter how true a vision from God may be, it will never be fulfilled in the manner in which we have imagined. All our expectations are incomplete. In fact, our very ideas often become the most subtle obstacles standing between us and our appointed future in God. Thus, we must keep our minds open and submitted to God, for when God fulfills His Word, it is always **"exceeding abundantly beyond all that we ask or think"** (Eph. 3:20).

In our last chapter we talked of Mary and her role as "Keeper of the Vision." Here, we will discuss how the Lord must shift our identity from control to complete surrender.

Interestingly, the first stage in Christ's preparation of Mary finds Him resisting her. Before the Lord can bring any of us into a new phase of His will, He must dismantle that "sense of attainment" which often accompanies our old relationship to His will. It is a fact that many church movements, both in and out of denominations, began simply.

Hungry souls longed for, and found, more of God. Over time, as their numbers grew, success replaced hunger; people grew more satisfied with God's blessings than with His Presence. There is a profound difference.

The apostle Paul illuminates this phenomenon, using Israel as an example. He writes, **"But Israel . . . failed to reach their goal. And why? Because their minds were fixed on what they achieved instead of on what they believed"** (Rom. 9:31–32 PHILLIPS).

What happened to Israel is typical of us all. Without realizing it, we find ourselves relying upon what we have achieved. The Bible says that God resists the proud but He gives grace to the humble (see James 4:6). It is always His mercy which guides our gaze away from our attainments and back to the knowledge of our need.

Today, people from many streams of Christian thought are beginning to acknowledge their own personal shortcomings. The fact is, *we all need correction!* And the beginning of that process is found in Jesus resisting our pride and restoring to us a fresh hunger to know Him.

Thus, in order to ultimately lift Mary higher, Jesus must lower her opinion of herself: He resists her on her present level. It is interesting that, in response to His resistance, Mary's need to control seems to grow more aggressive.

> **And He came home, and the multitude gathered again, to such an extent that they could not even eat a meal. And when His own people heard of this, they went out to take custody of Him; for they were saying, "He has lost His senses."**
> —Mark 3:20–21

These are strong words: **"take custody . . . He has lost His senses."** It is likely that the prevailing influence over Christ's relatives has come from Mary. Has her unrest caused their unrest? The issue is not that Jesus has lost His senses but that they have lost control. For Jesus to take control, we must lose control. Revival is as simple as that.

We should be aware that, when the real Christ begins to unveil Himself to His church, He will first reduce us from being achievers to becoming followers again. The very power of Christ to heal, deliver, and work miracles is contained in the revelation of His Lordship. *Deny Him His sovereignty in your church and you deny your church His power.* He cannot be manipulated, bribed, or begged. Remember, Jesus did no miracle until He began to manifest Himself as Lord. From that time on, the only relationships He actively sustained were those which recognized and submitted to His Lordship over them.

The very next scene in Mark's gospel begins, **"And His mother and His brothers arrived"** (Mark 3:31). We can imagine that, outwardly, Mary is subtly but clearly in charge. Inwardly, she is probably troubled and insecure. Jesus, surrounded by a multitude, is told, **"Behold, Your mother and Your brothers are outside looking for You"** (Mark 3:32). The implied undertone is, *There is someone here with something more important than what you are now doing.*

In any other scheme of things, it might be right to honor one's family with special privileges, but not above doing the will of God. Mary is outside looking in. For what may be the first time in her life, she feels a spiritual distance between herself and her Son. We should see that the more we set ourselves to control another person, the less intimate we can be with them; for intimacy is found in vulnerability and surrender, not in control. Of all those near to Jesus, Mary and family have slipped the farthest away; they are *outside* the sphere of intimate fellowship.

When Jesus was told His mother had arrived, He took the opportunity to end this stage of their relationship by saying,

"Who are My mother and My brothers?" And looking about on those who were sitting around Him, He said, "Behold, My mother and My brothers! For whoever does the will of God, he is My brother and sister and mother."
—Mark 3:33–35

Though they were outside, they were close enough to hear His rebuke. Right there, the word spoken to Mary thirty years earlier by Simeon was fulfilled: A sword pierced her heart and her inner thoughts were revealed (see Luke 2:35). Christ surgically and mercifully removed from Mary the stronghold of control.

Today, God is surgically removing from us that which seeks to control Christ. It was for Mary's good that Jesus cut her off. It was for her gain that He destroyed that which unconsciously opposed Him. There are times in our walk with God that it is good for the Lord to cut off old attitudes which have limited His freedom to change us. If we are truly His disciples, we will not merely survive His rebuke; we will bear more fruit under His pruning.

As the day of His return nears, expect to see many changes. Our destiny is to become the body of Christ with Jesus as the head. The church was created to receive its directives from a living relationship with Him. There is no other way for us to be led by Him than through seeking Him in prayer and receiving His Word in contriteness of heart.

CHRIST AS LORD OVER ALL

Jesus is not being cruel when He terminates our efforts to control Him. Did He not command us, **"Whoever serves me must follow me"** (John 12:26 NIV)? Yet, with His command, was there not this promise, **"Where I am, my servant also will be"** (v. 26 NIV)? If we follow Him, we will

abide in fellowship with Him. His confrontation of efforts
to control Him is an answer to our deepest desires. We have
prayed and labored to see the real Jesus emerge through the
church—and He is! But He is coming as *Lord.*

At the same time, a caution is in order. This transition
is not a green light to usurp the authority of the pastor; this
is not an excuse to justify lawlessness in the church. If we
will all posture ourselves in prayer, ministering to Jesus as
Lord, as did the leaders in Acts 13:1–3, we are going to see
the most magnificent demonstrations of God's power and
glory.

If we want our Christianity to truly have Christ, we must
let Him rule. Certainly, there will be a thrusting of our lives
into greater dependency. Yes, we will be forced to embrace
the most drastic of changes. Without doubt, we will be
reduced to what seems like the beginnings of our walk with
God. Yet, we shall also regain the passions of our soul in
earnest seeking of the Almighty! And oh! How such seeking
pleases Him!

Biblically, this state of heart is called "first love," and
there is no reality of God in our lives without it. You see,
His arms are not short that He cannot reach to our churches
and cities. The privilege the Lord is granting us is to enter
the most profoundly wonderful, most unpredictably glorious, experience we can have: *to know the power of the
Living God!*

Reality is filled with meaning. What was once vague is
now a fulfillment of the Word of God! But it is also frightening.

There is something about the actual Presence of God
when He supernaturally interacts with mankind that has no
parallel in mere religion. It is a time of power but also of
great carefulness. Not only do the dead come alive, but also
the living may, as did Ananias and Sapphira, fall dead. It is
the most exultant, yet fearful, thing! Like the women at

Christ's tomb, it is a world filled with **"fear and great joy"** (Matt. 28:8). Such is our Christian experience when Jesus is Lord over His church!

What is perhaps most wonderful about serving the Lord is that, even when we fail and fall short, He remains true to His purpose in our lives. With Him, correction is not rejection. Although His hands wound, they also heal.

The end of our story about Mary is this: On the day of Pentecost, Mary and Jesus' brothers were all part of the 120 in the upper room. Scripture mentions Mary by name (Acts 1:14).

Mary truly proved herself to be a bondslave of the Lord. Here was this remarkable woman, humbled and broken but once again serving God on the highest level of yieldedness. What she wanted from the beginning, she obtained: *deep intimacy with Christ.* Yet, she reached her goal not by striving or trying to control Jesus but by surrendering to Him.

In the richest way, through the Holy Spirit, Mary again had Jesus living inside her. She learned the secret of being a follower, not a controller, of the Lord Jesus Christ in the day of His glory.

17

FOLLOW THOSE
WHO FOLLOW CHRIST

*"Brethren, join in following my example, and observe
those who walk according to the pattern you have in us.
For many walk, of whom I often told you, and now tell
you even weeping, that they are enemies of the cross of
Christ."* —Philippians 3:17–18

P aul faced a major problem in the first century: many
deceivers had crept into the Christian church. The
apostle said these false leaders were enemies of the cross of
Christ. Paul warned the Philippians to recognize the differ-
ences between a true man of God and a false teacher or
prophet. Without any sense of false humility, Paul declared
that both his vision and his attitude toward attaining it were
examples for us to follow.

The context in which Paul wrote describes both his self-
righteousness before he found Christ and his utter abandon-
ment of fleshly confidence afterward. We will study these
verses carcfully. For in an age of increasing deception and

distractions, we find a standard that will keep us aimed at the fulness of Christ's Presence.

BEWARE OF THE DOGS

Paul started this third chapter of Philippians with a caution. He said, **"Beware of the dogs, beware of the evil workers, beware of the false circumcision"** (Phil. 3:2).

There were three kinds of teachers Paul warned about. The phrase, **"beware of the dog(s)"** is still used today. It means there is a vicious animal here. Additionally, most of the dogs of Paul's day were scavengers. One could find dozens of dogs eating off the rubbish heaps outside cities in the first century; their faces would be bent downward as their muzzles turned up garbage.

Today's church has similar people: fault-finders— people without real faith or love who continually feed upon the garbage of life. Paul's warning holds true today: *Beware of those who whisper sarcasms to you, who are continually discovering what is wrong with others!* If you listen to them, their words will rob you of vision, leave you without joy, and drain you of your energy.

There are others who cannot accept God's promises of a glorified church at the end of the age. The idea of unity among Christians does not merely frighten them, it angers them. In spite of their criticisms, the expectation of a special time of glory at the end of the age was the apostolic viewpoint. Yet, so was the warning: **"beware of the dogs."**

Paul also warned against the evil workers. These are harder to discern than the "dogs," but he describes them briefly in the first chapter. They proclaim Christ from **"envy . . . strife . . . selfish ambition"** rather than out of love (Phil. 1:15–17). **"Beware,"** Paul said, of those who preach Christ to build their own kingdoms, whose ministries are motivated by ambition. James adds, **"For where jealousy and selfish**

ambition exist, there is disorder and every evil thing"
(James 3:16). In our nation, this has been a serious problem
in the church. May God help us all to preach Christ purely
from a heart of love!

The third warning was aimed against the **"false circumcision"** (Phil. 3:2). These were the Jewish Christians who,
when they were saved, tried to make Christianity an exten-
sion of Judaism. This last teaching was the most dangerous
because it seemed the most plausible.

The essence of this error was that Christ's atonement
was not enough for salvation; you also had to keep the
whole system of Mosaic Laws. Paul wrote the next fourteen
verses to refute these legalists, as well as to give the church
a clear example of what it means to be an authentic Christian.

THE TRUE PATTERN

**"For we are the true circumcision, who worship in
the Spirit of God and glory in Christ Jesus and put no
confidence in the flesh"** (Phil. 3:3). Paul explains that,
when it came to the righteousness in the Law, he had been
blameless. After presenting all the things of which his flesh
could boast—born of the tribe of Benjamin, a Hebrew of
Hebrews, a Pharisee, and a persecutor of the church—Paul
then states, **"But whatever things were gain to me, those
things I have counted as loss for the sake of Christ"** (Phil.
3:7).

In the apostolic definition of Christianity, truth is found
in knowing Jesus. We do not keep the Law—we keep Jesus.
Without violating the spirit of the Law, if we truly keep
Jesus, we will go far beyond the righteousness of the Law.

Paul said he counted **"all things to be loss in view of
the surpassing value of knowing Christ Jesus my Lord"**
(v. 8). Everything Paul may have been in his flesh he
considered as waste in order that he might gain Christ.

Christ was more than the Law-giver. He was the Faith-giver, Love-giver, Life-giver, Power-giver, and Health-giver as well.

Paul went on, **"that I may know Him, and the power of His resurrection"** (v. 10) If we say we know Him but do not know the *power* that raised Jesus from the grave, we really do not know Him as He is. In Acts, Peter proclaimed that it was *impossible* for death to hold Jesus (Acts 2:31). Hebrews tells us that Christ was raised as a priest by virtue of an **"indestructible life"** (Heb. 7:16). To be intimately acquainted with Christ's resurrection life as a source of *our* life is to know one side of Christ's nature.

Paul also embraced **"the fellowship of [Christ's] sufferings, being conformed to His death"** (Phil. 3:10). The knowledge of Christ's power is accessible only through conformity to His death; resurrection is attained through crucifixion. No one will enter the fulness of Christ's Presence without carrying the cross to get there. It is self which occupies the heart, denying Christ's entrance into our lives. Without the cross, self becomes our God.

Participation in Christ's sufferings is part of knowing Christ. Paul did not embrace death in a morbid surrender to destruction, He embraced *Christ's* death, the death to self. It is this surrender to God's will which manifests the Presence of Christ within us. It forgives those who have "crucified" us—a sacrifice of love, not merely self-denial.

In knowing Christ, Paul hungered to know both aspects of Christ: His sufferings and His resurrection. Hunger to know Jesus is part of the pattern of a true Christian.

Paul continued, **"Not that I have already . . . become perfect, but I press on in order that I may lay hold of that for which also I was laid hold of by Christ Jesus"** (Phil. 3:12). Keep this thought in mind: *This was an apostle who was pressing on!* This was a mature Christian who was reaching forward.

Paul said, **"One thing I do: forgetting what lies behind and reaching forward to what lies ahead, I press on toward the goal for the prize of the upward call of God in Christ Jesus"** (Phil. 3:13–14). What did Paul choose to "forget"? He put aside the wounds, the offenses, and the pains of yesterday that he might be fully given toward the upward call of God in Christ. *As long as we are continually remembering the past, we cannot leave it.* We disqualify ourselves from embracing the future God has for us!

The prize in true Christianity is to attain the glory of God. To obtain that prize is worth letting go of everything else. Those who would have you passively sit back with a false security are blind to the *goal,* the *prize,* the *upward call of God* into which Paul himself was pressing.

Many teachers will come and go throughout your life. As you seek guidance, remember Paul's warnings: *never follow anyone who is not himself pressing toward the prize of Christ Jesus!* You can pray for them, stand with them, and encourage them. But if they are not going where you are going, do not follow them!

Paul went on, **"As many as are perfect, have this attitude"** (Phil. 3:15). It was in this context that Paul said, **"Brethren, join in following my example, and observe those who walk according to the pattern you have in us"** (v. 17). Of course, the first and final pattern for our lives is Jesus Christ. Yet, Paul was the pattern of one in pursuit of the Perfect Pattern.

In this world of illusions, deceptions, and seductions, let us beware of those who are like dogs, always focused upon the refuse of life. Let us flee from the evil workers who are full of envy and ambition. Let us not yield to the legalists who put a standard of righteousness before us other than Christ.

Paul tells us that these all are **"enemies of the cross of Christ, whose end is destruction"** (v. 18–19). Let us, instead, run toward Christlikeness. Like Paul, let us press toward the glorious prize: laying hold of Christ Jesus our Lord. For it is here that the Presence of Christ manifests within us.

18

THOSE WHO
STAND BEFORE GOD

The position of standing before God is the highest service we can attain in the outworking of the Lord's purposes. God wants to teach us how to stand in His Presence.

THE PLACE OF POWER

No doubt each of us will soon realize our limitations in serving God on our current level. We simply must have more of His fulness: clearer instructions, greater power, more perfect love. These resources can be found in no other place but the Lord's Presence. The frustrations we feel at times are actually God's way of discouraging us from attempting to do His will without the empowerment of His Presence.

But let us be assured. At the end of the age, there will be a place of power, of rest, of abiding in Christ where we literally hear and serve the King of heaven. The relationship of which I speak is a place where God Himself works through us. To stand before the Lord is to enter that place.

There are various levels of standing before God. You can stand before Him for your family, church, community, or nation. Wherever He positions you, your task will be to represent Him as one sent by Him with His mission and His message. Your role will be to pray for those whom God has placed on your heart and talk to them when the Lord has something to say.

As the days unfold, not only will we know the Presence of the Lord in the most wonderful ways, we will know His voice. For what servant is there who cannot understand what His master requires? Thus, we can expect the Lord to make His will known in the clearest of ways, actually requiring each of us to personally hear His voice.

To stand in His Presence and hear His voice is our objective. Consequently, let us ascend in worshiping faith until we enter the fire of God's glory. Here, He will teach us to be quiet and stand—without anxious thoughts directing our attention elsewhere. As servants, we will wait upon Him until He speaks to our hearts.

At the same time, this does not mean we do nothing with the rest of our lives. As we learn to recognize His Presence and His voice, we must also remain faithful in little things. Although we are faithful in our responsibilities, we must not be distracted by them. Something greater is coming, something of which our faithfulness in little things is the foundation and prelude.

THE HIGHEST PLACE OF SERVICE

Throughout the Bible, we read of men and women of God who stood before the Lord. As the return of Christ approaches, it shall be no different: God will again have those who stand before Him. He will have a people who represent Him in all aspects of human existence. They will hear the *unique* word He has to say to the world around them. On the surface many will appear to be homemakers or employed by the world; in truth, they will ever be serving God.

Thus, as an example to us, let us look at the lives of some of God's servants. As we do, we will gain insight into what it means to stand before the Lord.

"Now Elijah the Tishbite, who was of the settlers of Gilead, said to Ahab, 'As the Lord, the God of Israel lives, *before whom I stand,* surely there shall be neither dew nor rain these years, except by my word'" (1 Kings 17:1, *italics mine*). Again we read of this similar position in the discourse between the Lord's angelic messenger and Zacharias: **"I am Gabriel, *who stands in the presence of God;* and I have been sent to speak to you . . . words, which shall be fulfilled in their proper time"** (Luke 1:19–20, *italics mine*).

When we are sent by God to speak His words, those words shall be fulfilled in their proper time. The authority and confidence that come from having been sent by God have no substitute in mere religion.

The Scriptures identify those who stand before the Lord as abiding in the highest place of service which can be rendered to the Almighty. To stand before Him is to dwell in ever-increasing surrender, and thus availability, to God. He who stands before Him is the Lord's messenger, hand-picked and trained to relay the words, intentions, and acts of God to this world.

In the days of His Presence, God will have those who stand before Him. The Lord says,

> **"And I will grant authority to my two witnesses, and they will prophesy for twelve hundred and sixty days, clothed in sackcloth." These are the two olive trees and the two lampstands that**

stand before the Lord of the earth.
—Revelation 11:3–4

I have heard interpreters say these two prophets are either Moses and Elijah, or Enoch and Elijah, or John and Moses. God is going to send them back to prophesy at the end of the age.

I do not believe God is going to bring back the old prophets. To do so would justify the doctrine of reincarnation. Even if the *spirit* of one of these prophets were to minister to a soul from birth, like it did with Elijah and John the Baptist, the person might have similarities but would still be His own person. John the Baptist was not Elijah, though the "spirit of Elijah" ministered through him (see John 1:21).

The same God who raised up Moses and Elijah is, even now, preparing the two who shall be assigned their appointed task at the end of the age: they shall stand before the Lord with unlimited power.

And if anyone desires to harm them, fire proceeds out of their mouth and devours their enemies; and if anyone would desire to harm them, in this manner he must be killed.

These have the power to shut up the sky, in order that rain may not fall during the days of their prophesying; and they have power over the waters to turn them into blood, and to smite the earth with every plague, as often as they desire.
—Revelation 11:5–6

Yet it will not only be the two witnesses who prophesy. I believe the Lord will have many people who have passed the tests, learned from the trials, persevered through the demonic attacks, and overcome the personal weaknesses of their own soul. Having secured themselves in the Presence of God, they stand in peace as His servants. While their level of authority will not be in the range of the two witnesses, when they speak their words will come freighted with the power of God Himself.

A DESTINY IN HIS SERVICE

To stand before the Lord symbolizes the relationship one has with God. It does not imply that we have stopped kneeling. Nor does it mean we have developed a sense of congeniality or carnal familiarity with God. Jesus was standing before the Father while He knelt in prayer in the garden. Elijah was standing before God while he bowed seven times in prayer for rain.

Today there exists in the church a spiritual phenomenon known as being "slain in the spirit." The experience is taken from the example of those who fell under the power of the Lord in the Bible. It was predominantly an Old Testament manifestation. Except when the Lord appeared to Paul on the road to Damascus and then to John on the Isle of Pathos, this manifestation did not regularly occur in the New Testament. Nevertheless, it has its place in the Bible and also in the lives of many Christians today.

Yet, if we accept this experience as biblical, let us also submit to God's purpose in this manifestation. In nearly all the biblical examples of one *falling* before God, the experience was a prelude to a new *standing* before God. It came as part of a commission; it represented a new level of service to God.

Daniel, after meeting one of the Lord's angels, wrote,

As soon as I heard the sound of his words, I fell into a deep sleep . . . with my face to the ground. Then behold, a hand touched me and set me trembling on my hands and knees. And he said to me, "O Daniel . . . understand the words that

I am about to tell you and *stand upright.*"
—Daniel 10:9–11 *(italics mine)*

Daniel was "slain in the Spirit." Yet the immediate result was that Daniel was told to stand upright. Here we see the pattern: a man trembling in awe only to be raised up to stand before God.

Likewise, Ezekiel had a frightening unveiling of the Lord. The prophet says, **"And when I saw [Him], I fell on my face and heard a voice speaking."** What was it that the Lord told him? **"Son of man, stand on your feet that I may speak with you!"** (Ezek. 1:28–2:1)

In the unveiled glory of God it was impossible for Ezekiel to do anything other than fall. Likewise in the command to stand, it was impossible to disobey when the Spirit entered him. **"And as He spoke to me the Spirit entered me and set me on my feet; and *I heard Him speaking to me"* (Ezek. 2:2, *italics mine*)

God told Ezekiel to rise, to stand! There is a time when to fall or stay prostrate is an act of disobedience. Many of us keep returning to prayer lines to be "slain under the power." Perhaps we should find out what the Lord would say to us. Maybe God is calling us to stand for our families, neighbors, communities, or churches. I think we have cut short this phenomenon from its God-intended goal: to raise up people who stand before the Lord.

BEFORE THE RAPTURE

"Keep on the alert at all times, praying in order that you may have strength to escape all these things that are about to take place, and to stand before the Son of Man" (Luke 21:36).

Traditionally, this verse has been used to identify those who would be caught up to Christ in the rapture. But you do not need to pray to **"have strength to escape"** the rapture, for participation in the rapture is not based upon our strength but the summons of Christ's command. As we have mentioned, the phrase, **"to stand before the Son of Man [the Lord],"** in every other instance in the Bible spoke of the place of anointing and commissioning. It represented oneness with the power and purpose of God.

In the last hours of this age, the Lord will raise up individuals who not only enter His Presence, they will stand there in His service. It shall be their joy and destiny to fulfill the will of God at the end of the age.

Part Five

AN UNVEILED FACE

When Thou didst say,
"Seek My face,"
my heart said to Thee,
"Thy face, O Lord, I shall seek."
                    —Psalm 27:8

19

"TELL FRANCIS I MISS HIM"

If all these things are true and the glory of the Lord is going to increase, what shall we do in preparation?

We cannot attain the glory that is coming if we do not esteem the glory that is here now. At this very moment, the Presence of the Lord is accessible to each of us. Yet, to *enter* His Presence and abide with Him is God's goal for us. It is also the very thing Satan fights against the hardest.

The nature of this battle is not easily discerned. The enemy does not appear with fierce countenance; He does not threaten us with retaliation if we begin to seek God. Satan is far more subtle. He manipulates the *good* things of God's blessings to keep us from the best gift: God's Presence.

The devil has a willing accomplice in our fleshly nature. Solomon noted, **"Behold, I have found only this, that God made men upright, but they have sought out many devices"** (Eccl. 7:29). Our **"many devices,"** gadgets, and technologies, for all the convenience they provide, will not sustain us in the days ahead. *There simply will be no substitute for God.* Instead of having hearts full of God, we are full of desires for the things of this life.

Remember, Jesus warned:

Be on guard, that your hearts may not be weighted down with dissipation and drunkenness and the worries of life, and that day come on you suddenly like a trap; for it will come upon all those who dwell on the face of all the earth. —Luke 21:34–35

Too many Christians are simply dissipated and drained by the attractions and surpluses of our prosperous society. Let me assure you, most of these things are not evil in themselves, especially when accommodated in moderation. The deception is in our definition of moderation, for what seems like a modest lifestyle to us would be excess and luxury to ninety percent of the world.

Pursuing the pleasures of this world can become intoxicating. It is here where Satan's activity is most veiled. Instead of seeking God and being available for His will, many of us are entangled in debt and desire. Like the ancient Babylonians, ours is a **"land of images, and** [we] **are mad over idols"** (Jer. 50:38 AMPLIFIED). Many Christians are caught in a maze of distractions.

Idolatry is so familiar to us, we think it not strange! We actually call our sports and movie stars "idols." These individuals are, in turn, *idolized* by millions of followers. Yet, whatever we continually idolize eventually will demonize our lives.

It is in the midst of this great societal prosperity and a multitude of distractions that the Lord wants us to walk with a single mind toward His glory. Can we do it? Yes, but we may need to rid ourselves of our televisions, or at least fast from them for a month. If that is too much, deny it entrance into your mind for a week. The degree of difficulty in turning the television off is the measure of our bondage. If we cannot let it go, it is because we are its captive.

In a land where excess, ambition, and envy are the counselors of men, only those who abide in the simplicity of Christ are truly free. We must choose to make our portion in life the Presence of God.

Jesus said, **"Blessed are the poor in spirit, for theirs is the kingdom of heaven"** (Matt. 5:3). To be poor in spirit is to be free of hidden greed; it is to see and possess the kingdom of heaven.

If you are truly liberated from greed—if, indeed, you do not bow to mammon—God will begin to release His wealth to you. If your heart truly becomes the Lord's possession, He will begin to entrust to you His possessions, both heavenly and earthly. As you become Christ's slave, the earth will be your slave; it, too, will yield its resources for the purposes of God.

WEARINESS IN WELL-DOING

If Satan cannot distract you with worldliness, He will seek to wear you out, even using the good works you are doing for the Lord as a means of draining your energy. In fact, Daniel speaks of a time at the end of the age when the enemy will attempt to **"wear down the saints of the Highest One"** (Dan. 7:25).

God never intended for us to do His will without His Presence. The power to accomplish God's purpose comes from prayer and intimacy with Christ. It is here, closed in with God, where we find an ever-replenishing flow of spiritual virtue.

In the beginning of my ministry, the Lord called me to consecrate to Him the time from dawn until noon. I spent these hours in prayer, worship, and the study of His Word.

I would often worship God for hours, writing songs to Him that came from this wonderful sanctuary of love. The Presence of the Lord was my delight, and I know my time with Him was not only well-spent but well-pleasing to us both.

However, as my life began to bear the fruit of Christ's influence, the Holy Spirit would bring people to me for ministry. In time, as more people would come, I found myself cutting off forty-five minutes from the end of my devotional time. Ministry would extend into the night, and I stopped rising as early as I had.

Church growth problems began to eat at the quality of my remaining time; ministerial expansion, training younger ministries, and more counseling and deliverance crowded the already limited time I had left. Of course, these changes did not happen overnight, but the months and years of increasing success were steadily eroding my devotional life. In time I found myself in a growing ministry but with a shrinking anointing to sustain it.

One day an intercessor called who prayed regularly for me. He told me that during the night the Lord spoke to him in a dream concerning me. I was eager to hear what the Lord had spoken to my friend, thinking perhaps He was going to increase our outreach or maybe supply some needed finances. I asked Him to tell me the dream.

What the Lord said had nothing to do with the things that were consuming my time. He simply said, *"Tell Francis I miss him."*

Oh, what burdens we carry—what weariness accumulates—when we neglect the privilege of daily spending time with Jesus. I cried as I repented before the Lord, and I readjusted my priorities. No longer would I counsel people in the mornings. I would spend this time again with God.

Yet, I thought I might lose some of the people who had recently joined the church. These were people who had come specifically for personal ministry. I knew I would not have the same time for them as before, but I had to make my decision for God.

The next Sunday morning I announced to the congregation that my mornings were off limits, consecrated to God. "Please," I said, "no calls or counseling. I need to spend time with Christ." What happened next shocked me. The entire church rose and applauded! It seems they wanted a pastor who spent more time with God! They were tired of a tired pastor.

As we enter the days of His Presence, our primary activity will be to minister to Christ. Certainly there will be increased pressures. There will also be times of great harvest and spiritual activity. No matter what circumstances surround us, we must position ourselves first and continually in the Presence of God. For to miss our time with Jesus is to miss His glory in the day of His Presence.

20

"FOR DREAMS TO COME TRUE"

Just because we walk and talk does not mean we are truly awake. Zechariah was not sleeping when an angel roused him "as a man who is awakened from his sleep" (Zech. 4:1). Perhaps we too need to be shaken from our slumber to possess the promises of God!

In spite of all the signs, wonders, and warnings announcing that we are truly in the last days, Jesus also said there is a mysterious drowsiness that we have to overcome. Indeed, immediately after highlighting the various evidences of the end (see Matt. 24), He compares the church to virgins who **"all got drowsy and began to sleep"** (Matt. 25:5).

Virgins sleeping at the end of the age: It seems incomprehensible with all the signs in the heavens and wonders upon the earth, not to mention the increasing Presence of Christ. Yet this phenomenon is something we each battle: the tendency to become spiritually drowsy and lose our focus as we wait for the Lord's return.

There is a subtle activity of the enemy that dulls our perception and seduces our zeal. Our vision takes a backseat to other less important aspects of life. From the beginning, the voice of Satan has had this lulling effect on mankind. Eve's excuse for disobedience was, **"The serpent hath caused me to forget"** (Gen. 3:13 YOUNG).

This sense of spiritual forgetfulness, of drowsiness, is the cloud of blindness that we each must discern and overcome. It was in regard to this that the Holy Spirit spoke to my heart through the following dream.

There was a temple standing in an open field. My view of the temple was from its side, about 200 yards away. I could not see its front, yet it must have been completely open because great light flashed out from the inside; it pulsed like lightning, yet was solid like sunlight. The block of light issued straight out and I knew this light was the glory of God.

The temple was so close, I knew that with a little effort I could enter the glory of God. The Holy Presence was clearly within my reach.

There were also others directly in front of me that I recognized as people from church. Everyone seemed very busy. And while the temple and its light were visible and readily accessible to any and all, every head was bent downward and turned away from the light; each was occupied with other things.

I heard one voice say, "I have to do laundry." Another said, "I have to go to work." I could see people reading newspapers, watching televisions, and eating. I was sure everyone could see the light if they wanted to—even more sure that we all knew His glory was near.

There were even a few people reading the Bible and praying, but everyone maintained the distance between themselves and the place of God's Presence. No one, in fact, seemed capable of standing up, turning, and walking into His glory.

However, as I watched, my wife lifted her head and beheld the Lord's temple. She then stood and walked toward the temple's open front. As she drew closer to the light, a garment of glory formed and thickened around her; the closer she went, the more dense the light surrounding her grew until she stepped in front of the temple. She then entered completely into the Presence of God.

Oh! How jealous I felt. *My wife had entered the glory of God before me!*

At the same time I realized that there was nothing stopping *me* from approaching God's Presence—nothing except the pile of things to do and responsibilities that, in truth, ruled my life more than the voice of God.

Pushing the weight of these pressures from me, I determined to rise and enter the temple myself. But, to my great regret, as I rose up, I woke up!

The longing and disappointment within me seemed unbearable. I had been so close to entering God's Presence. How I wanted to enter the temple and be swallowed up in His glory!

I cried, *"Lord, why did You let me wake up?"*

The word of the Lord spoke deeply into my heart. He answered: *I will not have My servant's life fulfilled by a dream. If you want your dream to come true, you have to wake up.*

Today, God is calling us all to awaken to the reality of His Presence. The promises God gives us in the Scriptures must become more to us than dream-like realities reserved for the hereafter.

For this reason, the Scripture says, **"Awake, sleeper, and arise from the dead, and Christ will shine on you"** (Eph. 5:14). If we truly want Christ to **"shine"** upon us, we must arise from the distractions that entomb us in lethargy and spiritual darkness.

It is time to put away all that is permissive, and even what is permissible, and find what is permanent. If we want our dream of attaining His glory to come true, we must all wake up.

21

AN UNVEILED FACE

We will not find the glory of God by copying techniques or studying books. His Presence cannot be entered by following manuals, but by learning to follow Immanuel.

TO BE KNOWN FOR KNOWING HIM

In our immaturity, the church has sought to be known for many things. We have sought to be known for our uniqueness and particular emphasis. Some have sought to be known for speaking in tongues; others desired recognition through their buildings or evangelistic programs. Still others have publicized unique combinations of church government or a regular agenda of special speakers.

This desire for human recognition and significance has created many church traditions that are unbiblical. They have not only separated us from each other, they have separated us from God.

Today's disciples, however, will be known for just one thing: *They will be known for truly knowing Jesus.* His Presence—not just doctrines about Him but His very Spirit and likeness—will uninhibitedly accompany those who follow the Lamb.

Because their focus is upon Him and Him alone, God will ultimately accompany their lives with great power. They will lay hands upon the sick, and instantaneous healings will be common. These miracles will be but a minor reward to a life that majors on loving Jesus.

Our salvation is not based upon what we do but upon who Jesus becomes to us. Christ alone is our righteousness, our virtue, and our strength! As we minister, it has to be in Jesus' power, or we are actually wasting time. Our confidence has to be in Him and not in our own ability. We must be settled in the knowledge that, while all things are possible for those who believe, apart from Him we can do nothing.

THE SACRED PRESENCE

Our noble quest is to awaken from the sleep of our cultural traditions; it is to seek and find the living Presence of God. To each of us, the Almighty has a heavenly calling, an upward call into spiritual fulfillment.

Our hope is not based on speculation or unreasonable expectations. It comes to us directly from the Word of God:

Now the Lord is the Spirit; and where the Spirit of the Lord is, there is liberty. But we all, with unveiled face beholding as in a mirror the glory of the Lord, are being transformed into the same image from glory to glory, just as from the Lord, the Spirit. —2 Corinthians 3:17–18

This is the glorious hope of our calling: we each gaze upon Christ with an **"unveiled face."** Paul said, **"we all . . . behold . . . the glory of the Lord."** The plan of God includes *you and me,* not just apostles and prophets, visionaries and saints. The opportunity—the holy privilege—is to remove the veil that separates us from God's Presence. Our inheritance is to behold His glory.

The old covenant speaks of two veils. One was the thick curtain that separated the Holy Place from the Holy of Holies within the temple. In the Holy Place, daily sacrifices were offered in ritual obedience to God; but in the Holy of Holies dwelt His sacred Presence. Into this small room, the high priest entered but once a year on the Day of Atonement. It was a fearsome experience.

When Jesus died, this veil was rent in two from top to bottom. It signified the new openness that had been secured by Christ into the Holy Presence. The fact that it was torn from top to bottom tells us that Christ's sacrifice purchased us complete redemption. The urgency of the rending—that it tore at the *exact moment* of Christ's death—speaks to us of the Father's passion to receive us back into His family (Matt. 27:51).

However, there was another veil that Moses used to put over his face when he left the Presence of God. This was done at the request of a nation who could not bear to look upon God's glory, fading as it was from Moses' face. The need for this veil was also removed in Christ. No longer would God have one man who dwelt in the sacred place while the nation lived separate. The new covenant has made us a community of glory—**"But we all, with unveiled face behold . . . the glory of the Lord"** (2 Cor. 3:18).

But what exactly is a veil? It is something that hides what would otherwise be visible. As mentioned, our religious traditions that do not accommodate the Presence of God can become a veil. How terrible that the very things we are doing for God might be the obstacles that are keeping us from Him!

"Their minds were hardened; for until this very day at the reading of the old covenant the same veil remains unlifted, because it is removed in Christ" (2 Cor. 3:14).

How can we discern when our traditions have become a veil between us and God's Presence? Indeed, how can we break out of the false or cultural traditions that we have been taught to venerate and honor? The answer lies in the measure of our love for God's Word and the softness of our heart toward His voice. As we yield to His voice, our return to God begins.

"But whenever a man turns to the Lord, the veil is taken away" (2 Cor. 3:16). Right now, you are alone with God. The simple act of turning toward the Lord removes the veil.

The Scriptures tell us that no one can say "Jesus is Lord" except by the Holy Spirit. Say it:

Jesus, You are my Lord.

Turn your heart toward Him. Do not be afraid. Remember, the rending of the veil in the temple was His idea; He desires you to come near. The moment you turn your heart, **"the veil is taken away."**

Lord Jesus, forgive me for my many traditions. Especially, Lord, forgive me for living separate from Your voice. I take off the veil. I turn my heart to Your living Presence.

22

THE RIVER OF
GOD'S PLEASURE

To live for God is to be nourished by the nectar of heaven.

As the days unfold toward Christ's return, an increasing number of voices will clamor for our attention. There will be church programs and prayer strategies, activities and powerful movements. Signs and wonders will splatter the world, dazzling the mind of man. In this environment, we must find the place of God's pleasure. We must be intimately acquainted with that in which His soul delights.

Remember also, the days ahead shall increase in pressure and troubles; because iniquity abounds, the love of many shall grow cold. Is not the world in which we live, even today, stricken with cold love?

We must not conform to our environment; we must conform to Christ. He always chose to give God pleasure, even in the midst of conflict and cruelty. We must redeem our encounters with the difficulties of human existence. Let us identify them as opportunities to worship our God. Our

Christlike spirit toward adversities gives great pleasure to the Father.

We were not created to live for ourselves but to live for God. As it is written, **"Worthy art Thou, our Lord and our God, to receive glory and honor and power; for Thou didst create all things, and because of Thy will they existed, and were created"** (Rev. 4:11).

The key to lasting happiness and real pleasure in this world is not found in seeking pleasure itself but in pleasing God. And while the Lord desires that we enjoy His gifts and the people to whom we are joined, He wants us to know that we were created first for His pleasure.

A "LAY WORKER" FOR GOD

To His neighbors, Jesus was just a carpenter's son. Yet, before Jesus' public ministry began—before there were any miracles or multitudes—there was a quality in Christ that, even as a carpenter, swelled the heart of God with pleasure.

From His youth, the compelling vision of Christ's life was more than just becoming a good man. As magnificent as it was, His aim reached beyond even His commitment to sinless adherence to the Law. The life goal of Jesus Christ was to give pleasure to His Father. In truth, He only did the things that pleased God.

Thus, could Jesus have heard a more wondrous utterance than that which God Himself spoke at His baptism in the Jordan River? At the sound of the Father's voice, the heavens opened; the river of God's pleasure flowed to His Son: **"Thou art My beloved Son, in Thee I am well-pleased"** (Mark 1:11; see also Luke 2:52).

Remember, Jesus was still a "lay person" when the Father spoke to Him. He had not yet entered public ministry. *It was Jesus' life while a tradesman which increased the Father's bliss.*

To give pleasure to God is the purpose of our existence also. Jesus' ability to please the Father while working a secular job tells us God is looking for something deeper than theological degrees and correct doctrine. He is looking for our love. And in this, we also can please Him. Whether we are housewives, secretaries, or auto mechanics, in God's eyes, true ministry is not in what we do but in what we become to Him.

Jesus said it often: The Father sees in secret. Amazingly, it is from this very world of our hearts that the gaze of God seeks pleasure. And when He finds a soul who, as an act of worship, gives of himself or perseveres in prayer or suffers patiently or loves purely, the Father's heart is drawn to such as these.

Let us consider it deeply: *We can actually bring pleasure to God!* What a wondrous privilege! Since it is possible, let us not grope through life without knowing the things that please the Lord. Indeed, let us specifically isolate that one way above all others which touches the heart of God. Paul said that God **"was pleased to reveal His Son in me"** (Gal. 1:15–16).

The first and most essential pleasure to God is to see His Son revealed in our lives. No one, nor any thing, brings pleasure to the Father as does His Son. Every time we obey Jesus, giving Him access to this world, we please God. Each time Christ forgives or loves or blesses through us, the heart of God finds pleasure in our lives.

Jesus did only the things He first saw His Father do. As we enter into the depth of His Presence, let us also seek to know how, in every situation, we may reveal Christ. For in the love between the Father and His Son the river of God's pleasure flows.

Oh God, the thought that my life may bring pleasure to You is so high, I can barely believe it. Lord, look upon me as Your workmanship; create in me that which will most glorify You. Make my life an aroma of thanksgiving that ever brings pleasure to Your heart.

23

STANDING BEHIND OUR WALL

The sense of distance we often feel between Christ and ourselves is a deception. As we enter the days of His Presence, the Lord shall remove that falsehood. He promises, "In that day you shall know that I am in My Father, and you in Me, and I in you" (John 14:20).

The Scriptures tell us that Christ is the vine, we are the branches; He is the head, we are His body; He is the Lord and we are His temple. From start to finish, the Bible declares the Lord as not only dwelling in heaven but also existing perpetually in redemptive union with His people. The ever-present object of His activity is to guide us into oneness with Himself.

In this regard, for all that the Holy Spirit has come to establish in our lives, whether through virtue or spiritual gifts, His highest purpose is to lead us into the Presence of Jesus. The Holy Spirit labors ceaselessly to establish intimacy between ourselves and the Lord Jesus.

This intimacy fills the letters and words of the Bible with the heart throb of God. Like sheep, we actually hear the Shepherd's voice speaking to our hearts (see John 10:27). Think of it: Not only are we privileged to know what Jesus taught; He is so close we can discern the tone of His voice as He instructs us. This is heart-to-heart intimacy. He says,

I am the good shepherd; and I know My own, and My own know Me, even as the Father knows Me and I know the Father; and I lay down My life for the sheep.

And I have other sheep, which are not of this fold; I must bring them also, and they shall hear My voice; and they shall become one flock with one shepherd. —John 10:14–16

Jesus tells us that the union between Himself and our hearts is of the same quality and nature as what He possesses with the Father. He says, **"I know My own, and My own know Me."** How intimate is this relationship? It can be as deep and penetrating as the love between the Father and the Son. Jesus said we could know Him **"even as the Father knows Me and I know the Father."**

Yet, the sense of distance between ourselves and Jesus Christ persists. You may have prayed, *Lord, You said You are with us forever, but I feel alone. I cannot perceive You.*

If Christ is within us, how can we find the flame of His glory? In the Song of Solomon, this quest to find the place of His Presence is given wonderful expression. The bride says, **"Listen! My beloved! Behold, He is coming, climbing on the mountains, leaping on the hills! My beloved is like a gazelle or a young stag"** (Song of Sol. 2:8–9).

This is our Lord—full of vitality! He is climbing on the mountains, leaping on the hills. To see Him on mountains, though, is to behold His mighty works from afar.

We may know theologically that Christ is within us, but to live in a moment-by-moment sense of His Presence seems unattainable. We still ask, *Where is He in regard to me?*

Her proclamation continues, **"Behold, He is standing behind our wall, He is looking through the windows, He is peering through the lattice"** (Song of Sol. 2:9). At this very moment Christ is standing behind our "walls." The walls between us and the Savior are primarily the work of our independent fallen natures. We have barricaded ourselves behind fears and carnal attitudes; we are held hostage by sin and worldly distractions. Yet these walls can be eliminated.

Imagine that, even as you are reading, the Lord Himself has entered a nearby room. Suddenly, the room is vibrant and alive, shimmering with eternal life. Brilliant waves of radiant light, like sunlight, flood your surroundings. Then, that holy light passes into *you,* and the darkness that once shrouded your inner secret attitudes and lusts, lies and compromises, is gone. You see yourself as you are. You are fully exposed without a fig leaf of self-righteousness to hide you. And you know throughout all your being that the real Jesus is in that nearby room.

First question: *Would you enter the room?*

If you could not bring yourself to step into His Presence, what would be your reason? If it is because of shame, because you feel you have failed the Lord too many times, then your shame has become a "wall" behind which Christ stands. If fear keeps you distant, then fear is the thought-barrier between you and God. Perhaps it is an unrepentant heart that is keeping you from intimacy with Christ.

Remember, it is the pure in heart that see God (Matt. 5:8). If we repent of our wrong attitudes and sins; if, instead of shame and fear, we clothe ourselves with the garments of praise and salvation, the barriers between ourselves and the Lord shall be removed.

But there is a second question: *How would you enter Christ's Presence?*

It is my opinion that we would not pick up tambourines and dance unruffled into His glory. Nor do I think holy laughter will accompany us into the terrible blaze of the Holy God.

When history's greatest apostles and prophets beheld Him, His Presence caused each to fall as a dead man before Him. We may *leave* laughing and dancing, but when I consider approaching the room of His Presence, it would be with great trembling that I position myself before Him.

How can we break the sense of distance between ourselves and Christ? In the same way we would repent of sin and shame before entering the room, let us turn our gaze toward His living glory. In trembling obedience, let us enter the fire of His Presence for, in truth, He is closer than the room next door. He is, even now, standing behind our wall.

Lord Jesus, I remove the wall created by my fears, sin, and shame. Master, with all my heart I desire to enter Your glory, to stand in Your Presence and love You. Receive me now as I bow before Your glory.

24

"WITH THE GLANCE OF YOUR EYES"

"Who is this that grows like the dawn, as beautiful as the full moon, as pure as the sun, as awesome as an army with banners?" —Song of Solomon 6:10

In the previous chapter we asked, *If you knew the Lord was as near as the room next door, would you enter?* We also asked, *How would you enter?*

These same questions have been asked of many Christians. Most of us sincerely love the Lord and are thankful for all He has done. As a people, we are more comfortable celebrating what Jesus has done *for* us than accepting who He desires to be *to* us. We will dance before Him, sing of His victories, and teach of His mercies. Yet, rarely do we quiet our hearts and surrender to His Presence; we want Him without becoming vulnerable to Him. For us, it is enough to serve Him through the types and shadows of religion. But it is not enough for Him.

Many will say to Me on that day, "Lord, Lord, did we not prophesy in Your name, and in Your name cast out demons, and in Your name perform many miracles?" And then I will declare to them, "I never knew you." —Matthew 7:22–23

As awesome and liberating as it is to know what Jesus has done for us, until we actually give ourselves to Him our religion will never be more than a "history lesson" and a commitment to be good. I will say it again: it is not enough. *Jesus wants to also know us.*

You say, *But He does know us!* In His omniscience, He knows everything. But in His love, He seeks to know us as beings that choose to exist in a living union with Him. He has the right to our souls, our secrets, and our dreams. He wants the person we are when no one else is looking. Yet, He will not force Himself. This is not the way of love.

This interpenetration of our lives in Him and His life in us is the only destiny with which the Father is content. At the end of the age, everything short of oneness with Christ will appear as sin.

GOD IS LOVE

As I shared in the beginning of this book, I too know the fear of the Lord. It is the beginning of true knowledge. But I have also **"come to know and have believed the love which God has for us"** (1 John 4:16). God is love, and the apostle who fell before Jesus as a dead man on the Isle of Pathos now tells us, **"There is no fear in love"** (1 John 4:18).

The Lord knows our fear of Him is a strong deterrent from sin and a wonderful ally in walking uprightly. Yet, to draw near to Him we must know more than the fear of God; we must know His love.

God's love is perfect. John tells us that **"perfect love casts out fear, because fear involves punishment, and the one who fears is not perfected in love"** (v. 18).

When it comes to entering the Presence of God, it is to be expected that fear, guilt, or shame should seek to hold us hostage to sins. But as we believe in the love God has for us—in the brightness of His mercy—the shadows of our past cannot exist.

The Heart of God

He was actually standing, waiting behind our walls when I asked, *Would you enter His Presence?* He was peering through the lattice of our worldly entanglements when I asked, *How would you enter?* We know how we responded, but we do not know *His* heart. When you harbored the thought—even just the possibility—of coming closer to Him, something within His being responded. He says,

"You have made my heart beat faster, my sister, my bride; you have made my heart beat faster with a single glance of your eyes" (Song of Sol. 4:9).

Your glance, even if it was no more than the briefest anticipation of being with Him, made His heart beat faster. The King James Version reads, **"Thou hast ravished my heart, my sister, my spouse; thou hast ravished my heart with one of thine eyes."**

Jesus is not returning simply to destroy wickedness; He is coming for a bride. At the end of the age our task is not simply to prepare for the rapture or the tribulation but for Christ! You see, there is nothing more important to Jesus Christ than His bride, the church. He died for her. He lives to make intercession for her. His love proved itself capable and worthy of winning our full redemption. Our most noble task is to surrender to the love that reaches to us.

LONGING FOR JESUS

How shall we respond? I am thinking of Mary Magdalene's love for Jesus. Yes, here in the love Jesus has for Mary and her response again to Him we see flashes of Christ's love for the church.

Mary is at Jesus' empty tomb. The apostles came, looked into the sepulchre, and went away bewildered. But Mary lingered, weeping. It is noteworthy that Jesus did not immediately come to the apostles; He came first to a woman. It tells us Jesus responds to love more than position; He comes first to those who want Him most. The apostles went away wondering, but there was something in Mary's inconsolably broken heart that Jesus Himself was drawn to.

In her sorrow she did not recognize Him. He said, **"Woman, why are you weeping? Whom are you seeking?"** (John 20:15) Blinded by her tears, she supposes Jesus is the gardener.

> **"Sir, if you have carried Him away, tell me where you have laid Him, and I will take Him away."**
>
> **Jesus said to her, "Mary!" She turned and said to Him in Hebrew, "Rabboni," (which means, Teacher). Jesus said to her, "Stop clinging to Me, for I have not yet ascended to the Father."**
> —John 20:15–17

The instant Mary sees the Lord she clings to Him. And here is the most astounding event: *Christ interrupted His ascent into heaven to answer this woman's love!* Jesus said, **"Stop clinging to Me. . . I have not yet ascended."**

In His next appearance, Jesus appears to the disciples. He tells them, "touch me." This manifestation is after He has returned from His journey into heaven—but for Mary, He broke the protocol. I am staggered by this: En route to the Father, Jesus stopped to respond to her heart.

This is the nature of His love. *His passion for His bride rules His every thought and action!* Our preparation for Jesus—our cleansing and coming into His glory—is the highest place of obedience we can offer God. *We* are the **"joy set before Him"** (Heb 12:2). For us, He despised the burden of humiliation and shame; He endured the cross. In so doing, Jesus demonstrated that His love for the church is the highest, most powerful law of His kingdom!

It is His passion for the church that compels Him to come for us in the rapture. Yet, as He broke "protocol" for Mary, so He reveals His heart. *If we will be satisfied with nothing less than Christ, it is Christ we shall possess.* He will come to us. Of all the marvels in this universe, the greatest is the love Christ has for His church. He is the source of her glory in the days of His Presence!

Oh Lord Jesus, forgive me for using Your gifts for myself, while withholding myself from Your love. Lord, I will love You with a perfect love, for my love is the love with which You first loved me.

NOTES

Chapter 2

[1]When we use the word *glory*, we are referring to the manifestation of the Lord's actual Presence. In the New Testament, this word, *doxa* in Greek, meant (a) "the self-manifestation of God, i.e., what He essentially is and does"; (b) "the character and ways of God as exhibited through Christ to and through believers"; (c) "the state of blessedness into which believers are to enter hereafter through being brought into the likeness of Christ"; (d) "brightness or splendor," (1) "supernatural, emanating from God (as in the Shekinah glory, in the pillar of cloud and in the Holy of Holies" (Vine's Expository Dictionary).

In the Old Testament, the Hebrew word for glory was *kabod* and it meant "weight, heaviness, or honor." When we speak of the glory of the Lord, we mean all of the above. As we draw near to the Second Coming, there will be an increasing "weight" of Christ's Presence manifested in the overcoming church. The splendor will be directly attached to the self-manifestation of God and the character and ways of God as exhibited through Christ to and through believers.

Chapter 6

[1]The book of Daniel speaks of an overall period of seven years in which the ministry of the Messiah is fulfilled. Considering the three and a half years of Christ's first advent, one common view is that the world will be in tribulation for 42 months. The other common view is that a full seven years of judgment awaits.

[2]For an insightful view into God's purposes with Israel and the church, the reader is encouraged to read *One New Man* by Reuven Doron.

[3]Taken from *The Lion Handbook to the Bible* (pg 75).

Chapter 8

[1]Whenever I use Old Testament references, I am aware some feel that verses spoken specifically about Israel should be limited to Israel. Others believe what once pertained to Israel has now become property of the church. My view (and use) of Old Testament prophecies is that they apply both to the nation of Israel and to the spiritual Israel, the church. Paul tells us, "For as many as may be the promises of God, in Him they are yes" (2 Cor. 1:20). This does not negate that God will also fulfill His eternal plan with natural Israel. Our fulfillment in

Christianity is primarily spiritual, whereas Israel's fulfillment is on a more physical plane.

Chapter 9

[1]Concerning the Parousia, except for literal translations, most English Bibles render both words as "coming" (Bibles with margin references will often place the word *presence* or even *Parousia* in the margin). Most Protestant commentaries as well as Catholic tradition identify the entire time period known as the Second Coming as the Parousia. Because the Parousia actually refers to the entire season of divine activity at the end of the age, the word is much more expansive in meaning than just identifying the calendar day of Christ's return.

Vine recognized that the contextual use of the word *Parousia* varied somewhat throughout the New Testament. It could identify the entire period of supernatural events that spanned the end times, or it might give prominence to a certain phase of the final days. Dr. Vine believed the Parousia would begin at the rapture and continue through the entire tribulation period. However, Bible teachers are divided concerning the timing of the rapture. In fact, many scholars find sufficient scriptural evidence to support either the "mid-" or "post-tribulation" rapture of the church.

QUESTIONS

Q: Is every Christian going to display God's glory at the end of the age?

A: In my opinion, everyone who truly longs for Jesus will have the richest measure of His Presence. I realize, though, that many Christians who have given their lives to the Lord did so from a fear of missing heaven. To attain the glory of the Lord is a reward for those who overcome. They will love Christ with an ever-increasing surrender of their heart, mind, soul, and strength.

Q: How does this teaching compare with the teaching about the manifestation of the "sons of God?"

A: The idea of "manifest sons of God" comes from Romans 8:19, where Paul tells us that **"creation waits eagerly for the revealing of the sons of God."** As I understand that doctrine, those who believe they are manifest sons also believe they cannot sin or die. Plainly, the context of the Scripture explains when this "revealing" would occur: **"And not only this, but also we ourselves, having the first fruits of the Spirit, even we ourselves groan within ourselves, waiting eagerly for our adoption as sons, the redemption of our body"** (Rom. 8:23). The "redemption of our body" will not happen until after we are changed in the rapture. Until then, as long as we are in this mortal flesh we will fight sin, sickness, and death; creation will continue in its subjection to futility and vanity.

Q: Are you saying the Presence of the Lord will take the place of the rapture?

A: The day of Christ's Presence is not a doctrinal substitute for the rapture of the church. The Lord Himself, in His glorified body (not just His Spirit), shall physically return to the earth both to receive His church and to judge the world. What I have to say leaves everything you believe about the rapture intact, whether you believe in the pretrib-, midtrib-, or post-tribulation gathering of the saints to Christ.

Q: Will we receive glorified bodies prior to the rapture?
A: No. Our physical bodies will still be susceptible to aging and corruption. Yet, at the same time, the Bible references nearly 400 instances where the glory, splendor, or majesty of the Lord are mentioned.

No one would think it was unscriptural to say that Moses actually beheld God's glory or that the Lord's glory shone from Moses' face. Neither do we debate whether Israel saw God's glory on Mount Sinai or at the temple dedication. Millions of Hebrews saw with their eyes the glory of God. They saw it rest on a building, a mountain, and a man. That same glory is *in* us now.

In the same way people who are oppressed or demonized can actually exhibit a gloom or darkness in their countenance, so those whose spirits have been filled with Christ will increasingly exhibit His glory as we near the end of the age. The idea of the Presence of Christ manifesting in His people by a distinguishing light is not foreign to New Testament thought. One only has to observe the paintings of the early masters to see saints with luminous bands of light around their heads.

NOTES

NOTES

NOTES

NOTES

NOTES

NOTES

NOTES

NOTES